DEVELOPING CROSS CURRICULAR LEARNING IN MUSEUMS AND GALLERIES

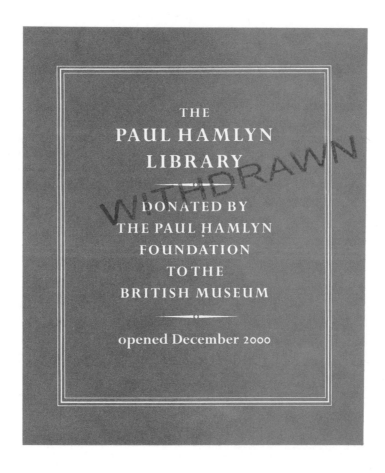

DEVELOPING CROSS CURRICULAR LEARNING IN MUSEUMS AND GALLERIES

Sue Wilkinson and Sue Clive

edited by Jennifer Blain

Work on this project was made possible by grants from
The Ernest Cook Trust, the Esmée Fairbairn Charitable Trust
and the Pilgrim Trust. It was carried out under the auspices of
Art & Society and South East Museums Education Unit.

Trentham Books

Stoke on Trent, UK and Sterling, USA

Trentham Books Limited

Westview House   22883 Quicksilver Drive
734 London Road   Sterling
Oakhill   VA 20166-2012
Stoke on Trent   USA
Staffordshire
England ST4 5NP

First published 2001

British Library Cataloguing-in-Publication Data
A catalogue record for this book is available from the
British Library
ISBN: 1 85856 236 8

Designed and typeset by Trentham Print Design Ltd., Chester and printed in Great Britain by Cromwell Press Ltd., Wiltshire.

iv

Acknowledgements

Thank you

to all the teachers, head teachers, advisory teachers, workshop leaders and artists whom we interviewed about case studies and who were so generous with their time

to staff at museums and galleries who supplied us with information and materials and especially to all those staff who gave up their time to talk to us about case study projects

to Eileen Adams, Martin Bazeley, Tim Benton, Frances Borzello, Michael Cassin, Nicky Durbridge, Chris Elmer, Eileen Hopper-Greenhill, Paul McKee, Margaret O'Brien, Anandi Ramamurthy, Jo Stockham, Marcus Tate, Myna Trustram, Caroline Wilkinson and Jane Wood who contributed so generously to the focus group days

to Emma Webb and Jane Middleton who helped us with the case studies

to the Esmée Fairbairn Charitable Trust, the Ernest Cook Trust and the Pilgrim Trust.

Contents

vi

List of Illustrations

1

Introduction to this book

'I rlly lickt the crab and I injoeyed the bager but the bets is the snake' (Anthony, Year 1, describing his visit to the SEARCH centre at Gosport)

Museums and galleries are wonderful places to take children to learn. Through access to real objects they offer experiences that help to stimulate curiosity, provoke questions, develop creativity and encourage independent investigation. Time and again during visits, teachers will say that they had never expected an individual child to answer that question, come up with that idea or produce that particular piece of work. It is clear that working with collections can help to motivate children and to build the confidence and self esteem they need in order to learn effectively.

The decision to seek funding for a book on cross curricular learning in museums and galleries emerged from research done by both the South East Museums Education Unit (SEMEU) and Art and Society into the use that educators make of collections. It was clear that, despite the good work which was being developed in some museums and galleries and despite the potential of the collections for teaching a wide range of curriculum themes, most educators were primarily using museums to support their teaching of history and galleries to support their teaching of art.

This book is designed to help educators in schools, museums and galleries to get the most out of local exhibitions, collections and displays and give them a fund of ideas that they can apply and also a methodology to help them to develop effective programmes for their students. It looks at ways of using school visits to develop cross curricular projects that are fun and educational for all involved and which will support a range of curriculum topics. The authors are both ex-teachers and have made sure that their suggestions are truly practical.

What makes this book different is our research into ways of using collections to support cross curricular learning. We set up focus groups with carefully selected specialists (many of whom were also educators) from a range of related fields such as art, history, science, design, photography and archaeology We put them in front of objects and paintings and asked them to brainstorm different ways of looking at the sorts of objects and images which teachers might find in their local collections and exhibitions and at the issues that would have to be considered when planning to develop cross curricular themes. What emerged was a plethora of different ideas and approaches. It was clear that each of these specialists looked at the objects in different ways. They saw different things. They made different connections. It was a powerfully creative process which made all of us realise that working on one's own to develop subject-specific programmes and resources (as many of us currently do) means ignoring the full creative potential of collections and exhibitions.

2

In addition to running focus groups we decided to search for case studies that demonstrate how museums and galleries have been used to resource cross curricular themes. The 13 case studies reported in Chapter 4 therefore feature actual examples of museum and gallery practice. Quotes from them appear throughout the book and give examples of the ways in which teachers, museum and gallery educators and students have enjoyed working with collections and exhibitions to support a variety of different learning objectives.

The case studies included in the book are:

Art and Dance a dance workshop for secondary school students exploring an exhibition by the artist Shirley Sully

Back to the Future was set up for key stage 3 students. It used buildings to explore how science and technology have changed life in the 20th century

Braque a project for students at a bilingual school which used the exhibition *Braque, the Late Works*, to support the teaching of modern languages and art

Casting Shadows an art and story-telling project for key stage 2 students which looked at everyday objects. Students worked with practising artists and displayed their work in their local gallery

Greek Vase a summer literacy project which used Greek objects to explore the theme of the Grand Tour

In Touch with the Past a project which used archaeological collections with key stage 2 students to look at craft and technology

Splash! a project by and for three to five year olds exploring the theme of water through paintings

Strike a Light a science project for key stage 2 students. It used social history collections to explore the theme of light

Swansea at War a Second World War project for students at key stages 2 and 3

The Egyptians was intended for secondary school students. It used Egyptian collections to study art and technology

Who's Been Framed? was a project for teachers, which looked at ways of using portraits to support history teaching

William Morris a music and English project for key stage 3 students which used the life and work of William Morris to stimulate creativity and composition

Words and Waves was planned for key stage 2 students and used an exhibition of photographs to support work in English and geography

We hope that readers will find that this book offers them ideas, strategies and approaches that can help them to make the most of the learning opportunities that museums and galleries can offer. Above all else, though, we hope that it will stimulate people to visit their local museum or gallery and start developing their own ideas for new and exciting ways of using those resources.

3

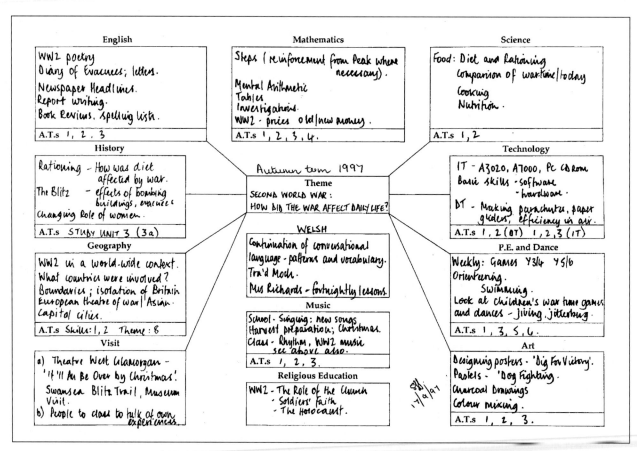

English

WW2 poetry
Diary of Evacuees; letters.
Newspaper Headlines.
Report writing.
Book Reviews. Spelling lists.

A.T.s 1, 2, 3.

Mathematics

Steps (reinforcement from Peak where necessary).

Mental Arithmetic
Tables
Investigations.
WW2 - prices old/new money.

A.T.s 1, 2, 3, 4.

Science

Food: Diet and Rationing
Comparison of war-time/today
Cooking
Nutrition.

A.T.s 1, 2

History

Rationing - How was diet affected by war.
The Blitz - effects of bombing buildings, evacuees
Changing Role of women.

A.T.s STUDY UNIT 3 (3a)

Theme

Autumn term 1997

SECOND WORLD WAR:
HOW DID THE WAR AFFECT DAILY LIFE?

Technology

IT - A3020, A7000, PC CD ROM
Basic skills - software
- hardware.
DT - Making parachutes, paper gliders, efficiency in air.

A.T.s 1, 2 (DT) 1, 2, 3 (IT)

Geography

WW2 in a world-wide context.
What countries were involved?
Boundaries; isolation of Britain
European theatre of war/ Asian.
Capital cities.

A.T.s Skills: 1, 2 Theme: 8

WELSH

Continuation of conversational language - patterns and vocabulary.
Tra'd Moth.
Mrs Richards - fortnightly lessons.

P.E. and Dance

Weekly: Games Y3/4 Y5/6
Orienteering.
Swimming.
Look at children's war time games and dances - jiving. jitterbug.

A.T.s 1, 3, 5, 6.

Music

School - Singing: new songs
Harvest preparation; Christmas.
Class - Rhythm, WW2 music
see above also.

A.T.s 1, 2, 3.

Visit

a) Theatre West Glamorgan -
'It'll All Be Over by Christmas'.
Swansea Blitz Trail, Museum Visit.
b) People to class to talk of own experiences.

Religious Education

WW2 - The Role of the Church
- Soldiers' Faith
- The Holocaust.

Art

Designing posters - 'Dig For Victory'.
Pastels - 'Dog Fighting'.
Charcoal Drawings
Colour mixing.

A.T.s 1, 2, 3.

Part of a topic web for Swansea at War. This was prepared by a teacher at Crymlyn Primary School, South Wales, and shows how he built cross curricular activities around a museum visit. (© John W. Rogers)

4

2

Why use museums and galleries for cross curricular work?

Museums and galleries can inspire children and bring the curriculum to life, developing new ways of thinking and learning and providing opportunities to express imagination and creative talents. (David Blunkett and Chris Smith in the government's response to *All our Futures ...*, 2000)

The strength of galleries as places of learning lies in their ability to change attitudes, evoke feelings, demonstrate processes, convey significant ideas directly and simply, and engage visitors personally and actively in ways that ensure that the experience is remembered long afterwards. (David Anderson, 1999)

Planning and running a visit away from school takes time, effort and resources – all of which are in short supply in most schools today. So, why do it? This chapter looks at some of the reasons for taking students out to museums and galleries and the ways in which they and their teachers can benefit.

Learning in a museum is different

Research into the ways in which people learn has demonstrated that they do so in a variety of different ways, depending on their cultural background, personal preferences and the current situation. Museums and galleries present different kinds of learning experiences. They offer the chance for students to practice and use all sorts of different skills. In even the most formal and old fashioned type of museum there are opportunities for looking, talking, recording, asking questions, problem solving, investigating, comparing, measuring, thinking, sorting and setting. In most museums and galleries today there will also be opportunities for handling, drama, role-play, experimentation, doing and making. All of these activities should be responses to real things. Museums and galleries offer students the possibility of engaging with other times and other cultures. Objects have the power to stimulate creativity and excitement but they are also a way of finding out more about the people who made and used them.

Our case studies indicate that teachers valued the range of different learning outcomes that were offered their students. A teacher from *In Touch with the Past* commented particularly on the opportunities it gave her students to work with real objects *'direct experience bypasses the need for theorising and conceptualising ... The visit helped to develop students' enquiry skills'*. A teacher who had brought a class to *Back to the Future* thought that it provided real motivation for those students who found classroom science difficult or uninteresting. The buildings and the domestic objects used to create room settings in the museum provided students with an everyday context for their science-based work and encouraged them to ask more questions.

Museums and galleries also offer teachers the opportunity to take their students into a very different learning environment. They can provide flexible working spaces which can be used in a variety of ways. Learning can take place formally or informally, individually or in groups.

Some students like peace and quiet

> *Being there I liked the peacefulness of the collection and in the room I picked I was the only person in the room and I was thinking all I could hear was the ticking of the clocks. I wouldn't mind coming here again.* (Quoted in Norman Binch and Liz Roberson, 1994)

Whilst others have commented on the value of group work

> Jamie: *If I went with a group it would probably be easier, but if I went by myself I'd be out of place...*

Jason: *By myself, I'd spend two minutes in there. But like with a group you can figure things out...we was all sitting down there making answers or questions...*

Owen: *Yeah, you discuss it...* (Norman Binch and Liz Roberson, 1994)

The magic of objects

In May 2000, the Department for Culture, Media and Sport (DCMS) and Department for Education and Employment (DfEE) published *The Learning Power of Museums – a vision for museum education*. It says that more could and should be made of the educational potential of museums and that museums have the capacity to inspire and support a learning society. It goes on to say that education should be at the heart of every museum whatever its size, origin or ethos and that '*a museum's outlook, priorities, planning, presentation and facilities ... need to reflect the importance of learning, and education needs to feature prominently in mission statements, strategies and forward plans*'.

That museum objects are powerful tools for learning has been acknowledged for many years. In 1992, Her Majesty's Inspectors noted that

> *Giving students access to resources not available in schools helped them to develop knowledge, understanding and a range of skills particularly in English, technology, history, art and other cross curricular issues.* (A Survey of Schools' use of Resources, 1992)

and the first National Curriculum urged history, art and also design and technology teachers to use museums and galleries with their students. Each new version of the curriculum has included similar references and Curriculum 2000, with its new emphasis on values, key skills, thinking skills, inclusion and citizenship, is no exception. Curriculum 2000's programmes of study have been organised to point out the kinds of cross curricular possibilities which the teachers who feature in our case studies were developing through their projects.

The Qualifications and Curriculum Assessment Authority have a unit called *Visiting a museum, gallery or site* in their scheme of work for *Art Design,* and this acknowledgement of the role visits to collections and exhibitions can play in the learning process is, after a gap

7

of years, something that OFSTED is also going to be looking at. The subject advice for OFSTED inspectors acknowledges the role that collections can play in the learning process. It urges inspectors both to look at the use that schools make of museums and galleries and also to examine how the work that students have done on site feeds into the work being done in school.

Many of our case studies illustrate the power of objects in this respect. After looking at the significance of everyday kitchen objects in the case study *Casting Shadows*, one student wrote '*I thought the whole project was brilliant, excellent and exciting*'.

A member of one of our focus groups said

> *Kids sometimes with paintings or objects go 'Wow!' There is the mystery of something. How you decipher that, I don't know. Even if all you do is make people aware that it is there and it is original. Yes, there's perspective and it's clever. Yes, there are luscious uses of paint. Yes, there is rhythm like a dance. Yes, there is complexity like a piece of Bach. You can do all that, but it still doesn't get over that there is something bigger than all these things.*

8

Objects can have a long term impact on teachers and students as some of our case studies show. As a result of *Who's Been Framed?* the teacher developed a half term's scheme of work on the Tudors for Year 8 students and also changed her approach to teaching the Victorians in Year 9. As a direct consequence, she intends to incorporate a visit to look at portraits into her new schemes of work. In the year following *The Egyptians* project, one student, during a controlled test which required her to make two related masks, went back to her earlier project and made masks which were completely her own work but which drew again upon her experience at the museum. Teachers who visited the *Greek Vase* summer literacy project were also determined to use the museum again in future programmes.

Learning in museums is fun

> The combination of leisure and learning that museums can offer is a most valuable asset ... We know that experiencing real objects and creating their own work can make a lasting impression on children. (Chris Smith and David Blunkett in the foreword to *The Learning Power of Museums ...*, 2000)

The report *Children as an Audience for Museums and Galleries* (1997) found that children are attracted to museums and galleries because they offer '*a unique combination of opportunities to learn and have fun at the same time*'.

Fun is something most teachers value; they see it as an important part of the learning process. SEMEU carried out a survey of schools in Hertfordshire in 1996 and asked teachers what, amongst other things, they wanted from taught sessions in a museum. They wanted access to real objects, activities for children, the opportunity for students to ask questions and to find things out for themselves and for their students to have fun. They saw this as something which museums and galleries could offer their students.

The teacher whom we interviewed about *Who's Been Framed?* said that she found the idea of using portraits as evidence attractive and fun and she enjoyed developing skills in interpretation, analysis and communication with her students. This is backed up by the response of many students to the experience of looking at and handling objects, attending workshops and making objects based on their experiences.

Museums and galleries can offer students experiences which they cannot get in the classroom and which they enjoy and value. As a conclusion to the *Words and Waves* workshop, the students were asked to do a small piece of 'think writing' about their experience in the gallery. The workshop leader found that they had very much enjoyed talking and sharing ideas about the photographs both with their peers and also with her as a writer.

It is not just teachers and students who see museums as places which can make learning fun. SEMEU also carried out research into what families want from museums for the London Transport Museum in 1997. Those findings showed that adults want an experience that is fun as well as educative both for themselves and their children and that they are getting it in museums.

Support for teachers

Many museums and galleries now have a professional educator on the staff whether building-based, as in *Greek Vase*, or freelance, as in *Words and Waves*. The teacher involved in *The Egyptians* commented '*It is beneficial for students to get out of the school environment and work with someone fresh. They are stimulated and given ideas, and they remember what she tells them*'.

> *Our case studies also show that students benefit from working with a different person 'They also learned to concentrate ... The students were transfixed. As I approached them they were totally unaware of me ... She had confidence in them. She made them blossom. She got a quick response'.* (Head teacher, Greek Vase)

Where there are professional educators on the staff they will help teachers to prepare and run their visit and they may offer direct teaching or handling sessions. They can save teachers' time by planning and setting up experimental materials and activities and providing background information. Even in museums without education staff there can be curators who are keen to work with schools and who are a source of specialist knowledge, information and expertise. A curator initiated *Splash!*

Museum and gallery educators can bring special skills to a project that a school is planning. One of our focus groups made the point that

> *'If you work with the same objects over a period of time you build up a set of responses to them. You know what might come out of them; you are used to using them. That is what is so fascinating about seeing museum education at work because it is so natural and spontaneous. But there are years of experience behind it and there are various flexible ways of going into it ... It is a building-up of expertise and knowledge, but it is also about communication. It is a relationship between the knowledge and the group you happen to be working with at a particular time and what their interests are and what time they have available. It is all very subtle and sophisticated.*

> *There has to be a balance between knowledge and experience of working with two kinds of raw material, the [visiting] group and [museum] objects. Teachers in the classroom have experience of dealing with the raw material in their classroom but less experience of dealing*

The museum education officer brought her own special skills to a summer literacy project, and students enjoyed the challenges of working in a different environment. See the case study *Greek Vase.*

11

with objects. Getting the balance between the two things in a connected way is very important'.

Museum and gallery staff may also employ teaching strategies in the gallery which might be new to teachers and engaging for students

I began by introducing the young people to the pictures and asking them to describe one of them. This is a technique I have used many times. I sit with my back to the picture and go round the group, each participant having to say something different about the piece until I look at it and we compare what has been said with what is there. From this starting point we can develop the discussion about colour, tone, composition, line, texture, form, movement and so on and begin to make links with the vocabulary of dance. (Museums officer, Art and Dance)

As well as offering whole teaching sessions, museum and gallery educators provide material for teachers, which can be put to different uses. For example, it may be used as preparation, as in the case of *Braque*, as follow up or even to inform the whole topic, as in *Swansea at War*. The organisers of *Back to the Future* intended their packs to provide '*all the materials that [science] teachers would need to incorporate the project into their programmes of study'*

Museums and galleries often provide or collaborate on support through professional development sessions. In many of our case studies, INSET was offered as part of the project. A teacher we interviewed about *Who's Been Framed?* which was a project specifically for teachers gave us a long list of the benefits she thought she gained. First, there was the opportunity for professional development through advice and inspiration from experts in history and art. Secondly, she enjoyed working with a wide range of teachers in both subjects. Thirdly, she mentioned the visits to inspiring places and the exciting resources made available. But, above all, she appreciated the opportunity to take the initiative back into her school.

However, museum and gallery projects themselves can help teachers develop their practice. Commenting on *Back to the Future* a teacher said that, together with the resource materials provided, it had introduced changes into his teaching style. Another teacher told how she was able to introduce a dance module for boys following her students' participation in *Art and Dance*. Yet another teacher, this time involved in *Swansea at War*, had used the museum visit as the basis for a whole term's project covering all aspects of the curriculum. *Splash!* was seen as providing support for the head of the nursery school in training both staff and parents in suitable approaches to art education for young children.

Museums and galleries also offer teachers from schools opportunities to share their expertise and to influence project and exhibition planning. In *Back to The Future*, for example, a self-selected team worked with advisors to develop ideas for the format, content and structure of the project. In response to teachers who had already visited *Strike a Light* with their students, additional objects and displays were provided including a prism display that could be used to demonstrate how light is made up from the seven different colours of the spectrum. The intention was to encourage teachers to introduce additional themes and ideas about light.

Support for teachers does not just come from professional educators or curators. Many museums and galleries now employ creative professionals such as artists, craftspeople and poets to work with schools and to develop workshops based around the collections. They may work in the museum or gallery or as Artists in Schools. As can be seen from our case studies, the opportunities for schools to work with visual artists, writers and performers is invaluable. As well as offering specialist knowledge and skills, artists can also bring fresh approaches to looking at objects and to cross curricular work. They can develop students' personal and social skills, introduce different cultural traditions and provide role models for students and support for teachers. Artists bring another dimension and excitement to the curriculum. As one student said '*It is exciting when you've been chosen to work with real artists. I am sad when it is the last time we get to work with real artists*'. (*Casting Shadows*)

13

There is one near you

There are over 2,000 museums and galleries in the United Kingdom. Over 1,000 are independent, about 800 are run by local authorities, around 300 are university museums and collections, 200 are armed services museums and 26, mostly nationals, are funded directly by the government. The majority of our case studies took place in local authority museums but one was initiated as an outreach project by a National gallery and one by a gallery attached to an academic institution. These museums and galleries vary in size, locality and prestige, but they offer a huge range of resources. They demonstrate that there is a museum with potential for cross curricular work within the reach of most schools. This book proves that while local collections can help students to understand their local environment and its history they can also be used to open up a world stage.

The museum habit

Taking students out to museums and galleries when they are still at school plays an important part in helping them to develop the 'museum habit'. If young people are introduced to the excitement of museums and galleries and learn to feel at home in them, it is likely that they will perceive them as a resource for life long learning. A MORI survey for the Museums and Galleries Commission carried out in March 2000 showed that one third of school children go back to the museums and galleries that they have visited with the school. (*Visitors to Museums and Galleries in the United Kingdom*, 2000).

This is illustrated by comments from our case studies and elsewhere.

It's amazing how many will come back (Teacher, The Egyptians)

They discovered that the museum was interesting and exciting for them and many made return visits bringing their parents (Head teacher, Greek Vase)

A   *It was a hell of a lot better than I thought it would be ...*

Q   *Do you think that now you have been there you are more likely to go to other galleries?*

A   *Yes, definitely.*

Q   *What do you think you have gained from that trip then, generally?*

A   *Opened my mind up to art basically, which made me want to go more, because again I was kind of roped in to going, I had no choice. But if I had had the choice I still would never have gone and would still be saying it really didn't interest me, so that's how I think it is for many young people, you have to be forced to go and then you will get into it.*
(John Harland and Kay Kinder eds., 1999)

Independent learning

Study Support activities help motivate young people and give them extra confidence to learn during their school days and beyond. *'The many activities which make up Study Support have in common the aim of creating well motivated, independent young people who will become lifelong learners'*. (David Blunkett in *Extending Opportunities ...*, 1998)

The power of objects to stimulate and support learning goes beyond classroom-based and formal education. This is why museums and galleries have been identified as places that can support effective learning for young people both outside the formal education system as well as within it. Some are being used as agencies in the government's Study Support initiative. In 1998 the DfEE funded 17 pilot Study Support programmes in museums and galleries. These projects were externally evaluated by Education Extra, the Foundation for after school activities. Their report noted that the pilot projects have *'shown how collections can be used creatively and imaginatively to stimulate young people's interest in their heritage, to build their confidence and to help them develop new skills and interest in learning'*. (*Alive with Learning ...*, 1999)

Research carried out in 1999 to look more broadly into the benefits of study support noted that it *'would seem to have a particular role in helping children from disadvantaged backgrounds and those in need of additional support with their learning'*. The report continued by noting that *'those who take part in a range of activities outside school are better motivated and achieve better results in school'*. (*The Benefits of Study Support ...*, 1999). The New Opportunities Fund is providing over £200 million until 2002 to support the development of more Study Support programmes and, following the success of the pilot programmes, many museums and galleries are now working with schools to develop programmes, activities and resources for young people.

As David Anderson, in the report quoted at the head of this chapter, says

> *The potential of museums to extend students' learning beyond the classroom is highly prized by many teachers ... The value of museums for schools is much greater than that derived from school trips alone. Museums are an essential part of the broad cultural context within which school learning develops.* (David Anderson, 1999)

15

Literacies

The changes to the national curriculum have placed more emphasis on numeracy and literacy in schools. Paulo Friere is a Brazilian theoretician who has done much work on combating illiteracy whether it is in the third world or in inner cities of the western world. He has written on the importance of communicating about the relationship between the world and the objects in it as powerful motivation for learning to read and write. As infants we learn to make sense of the world about us before we learn to read words. There is a constant relationship between our skills in interpreting what we see, experience and say and the ability to read. As we experience the world we rewrite it for ourselves so to speak.

For Friere, this practical rewriting is central to the literacy process. Friere goes on to suggest that, in the teaching of literacy, the words used should come from the learners

> *... expressing their actual language, their anxieties, fears, demands and dreams. Words should be laden with the meaning of the people's existential experience and not the teacher's experience...Reading always involves critical perception, interpretation and **rewriting** of what is read.* (Paulo Friere and Donald Macedo, 1987).

'Rewriting' might equally describe the kind of learning process which occurs in museums and galleries. Many of our case studies have shown the efficacy of building on students' own experience, language, extrapolated meanings and feelings. Literate young people are better able to make sense of their environment and operate effectively within it.

Museums and galleries provide many opportunities for improving literacy in this sense and, by the same token, students' visual literacy. Visual literacy might be defined in terms of '*a group of vision competencies human beings can develop by seeing and at the same time having and integrating other sensory experiences*'. (Quoted in Karen Raney, 1997).

In our case studies, students have used creative competencies to communicate to others through art, dance, writing, foreign languages and music. They have appreciated contemporary and historical photography, painting, decorative art, design and technology and the processes involved in making the objects they analysed.

Personal, Social and Health Education and Citizenship

Education of 'the person' in terms of self-confidence, ability to relate to others and experience of sharing ideas are often deemed greater ideals than achievements in a specific subject. Education of 'the person' is, after all, an aim which goes back to the ancient Greeks, and it has a long tradition of relevance to education.(Rob Barnes, 1993)

Personal and Social and Health Education and Citizenship is now high on the school agenda. In 2003 Citizenship will be a foundation subject for all 14 to 16 year olds.

Curriculum 2000 includes, for the first time, a detailed and overarching statement on inclusion and a more explicit rationale which sets out the fundamental principles underlying the curriculum and which looks at Values, Aims and Purposes. The guidance is explicit on the values which should be taught across the curriculum and these include spiritual, moral, cultural, social, physical and mental development. Museums and Galleries such as The Galleries of Justice in Nottingham have developed programmes based around citizenship themes.

Museums and galleries can be rewarding places for raising moral and ethical issues via discussions about why the objects are there, how they got there, how they have been interpreted over the centuries and also about the nature of the objects themselves. The art education officer for *The Egyptians* used the collections to provide opportunities to discuss different attitudes and beliefs about death in 20th century British cultures as well as to look at the meaning and function of Egyptian artefacts.

Our focus groups found the same thing. One group spent a long time discussing the issues raised by a suffragette display

We were saying there is a little story here. It is a bronze medal given by Emily Pankhurst to one of the suffragettes who slashed a painting in the National Gallery. Usually that kind of thing is seen as anti-heroic, to slash great works of art. There is ambiguity. When does an act become heroic and when isn't it? There are issues around 'How far would you go to support a cause?'

As well as helping to develop students' social skills and to stimulate them into talking about moral and ethical issues, museums and galleries can sometimes help to boost students'

17

confidence and pride in their achievements by publishing or exhibiting their work, as is demonstrated in four of our case studies. As one student said about the exhibition *Casting Shadows* '*I like the pictures on the wall and I like this gallery and my work is lovely in this gallery*'.

The pre-school children involved in *Splash!* demonstrated a growing confidence in decision making and some understanding of the role of the gallery and its audience. *Bondi Beach* by AN Pybus was their favourite picture and the children were very keen to make their own version of this as a wall hanging. They wanted their work to be properly displayed. They were especially keen to see it in a frame like the other paintings in the gallery.

During interviews for our case studies, many teachers referred to this aspect of learning and to its importance. They said that there had been personal and social benefits for their students. The teacher believed that students taking part in the *Greek Vase* project had gained in confidence. The teacher involved in *Casting Shadows* felt that it helped to improve his students' drawing and making skills, and also that it provided more intangible benefits such as an increase in self esteem. He also thought that an enhanced image of the school as a whole was helpful to students in an inner city area. '*They start saying the school is good, start behaving as if it is good. Tell them that they are good and they are good*'.

Learning in museums and galleries is on the learning agenda

In 1998, the DCMS published its comprehensive spending review – a process which government departments go through every three years. The starting point for the review was to link the department to the government's overall policy agenda. The review said that the future direction of the department lay within four central themes

Access for the many, not the few
Pursuit of excellence and innovation
Nurturing educational opportunity
Fostering creative industries

The review also stated that museums '*are about objects and for people*'. Museums and galleries are seen as playing an important part in delivering these four themes. They can

18

promote education and life long learning in the information society, provide physical and intellectual access to artistic, scientific, historical and contemporary collections and exhibitions, help to tackle social exclusion, inform commerce and business and regenerate communities which, in turn, support economic prosperity. Since then DCMS has worked with DfEE to produce a vision for museum education called *The Learning Power of Museums* which looks at the role that collections and exhibitions can play in encouraging and supporting learning.

Government policy and new funding opportunities aim to bring more young people into galleries and museums where they can develop the habit of enjoyable, independent learning. DCMS has developed an Education Challenge Fund to enable small museums to develop their educational capacity (DCMS and Resource, Education Challenge Fund, 1999-2001) and the DfEE has put £2.5 million into a three year (1999-2001) Museum and Gallery Education programme. Projects are being run in 55 museums and galleries and these all aim at encouraging closer collaboration between teachers, museum and gallery educators, artists and other agencies.

Using museum collections to support students' learning and to provide them with new learning opportunities is therefore very topical. Our case studies demonstrate different ways in which collections and exhibitions have been made accessible to students and how active, participatory ownership of projects and educational activity in public galleries has been encouraged.

At the launch of the third national Gallery Week on 17 July 1998, Chris Smith, Secretary of State for the DCMS called the event '*a noble cause*' because it offered young people the exciting experiences to be found in museums and galleries. He stressed that excellence, one of his four fundamental principals for the arts, should not be seen as the élitist excellence often attributed to museums and their contents but should rather be seen as the kind of excellence found in many education programmes offered in museums and galleries around the country. He also made the keynote speech at the conference '*Visiting Rights?*' at Tate Modern organised by the European Socrates project together with MUSAEAM and Cultural Trends, in June 2000. The minister's presence at these events marks a huge step forward in recognising the potential benefits of gallery and museum visits.

19

Access and inclusion

Access for All and developing strategies for a more 'inclusive' society are key government priorities. In 1998 the government set up a Social Exclusion Unit and 17 Policy Action Teams were established to develop policies across specific service areas which would look at ways in which they could tackle social exclusion. In 1999 Policy Action Team 10 reported on how to maximise the impact on poor neighbourhoods of government spending and policies on arts, sports and leisure and on best practice in using these as ways to engage people in poor neighbourhoods, particularly those who may feel most excluded. In April 2000 The Social Exclusion Unit published the results of this and the work of the other 16 teams in the report, *A National Strategy for Neighbourhood Renewal.*

These reports show the role arts and culture can play in developing people's skills, self confidence and self esteem, something which all our case studies have borne out, but they also make it clear how much has yet to be done. They urge local authorities to use arts, sports and leisure positively. In response to these reports, The Group of Large Local Authority Museums commissioned research (*Museums and Social Inclusion. A Report to GLLAM*, October 2000) to look how their museums were tackling social exclusion. The results of this research showed both the amount of work which is being done in museums but also the impact which museum and gallery programmes can have on both individuals and communities

3

The research for this book:
focus groups and case studies

The focus groups

The purpose of setting up the focus groups was to bring together people with a range of specialist skills and knowledge. We wanted to ask them to look at objects and think of ways they could be used for teaching across the curriculum.

Another aim was to pilot an approach to discussing objects which could be used as part of a whole school INSET session. We wanted to prove to ourselves the power of brainstorming as a tool for planning a cross curricular project in a museum or gallery. This approach is set out in Chapter 6.

We selected two London venues, Leighton House and the Museum of London, which could give access to their collections of objects and paintings. Although they were very different from each other, we tried to select objects, which might be available in any local museum or gallery.

We then got together two lively groups that included practising artists, a photographer, curators and museum and gallery educators, historians specialising in media and also art and design, educational theorists, teachers, university lecturers, scientists, and archaeologists. We asked them to spend the day looking at groups of objects and paintings and discussing both their own responses to them and ways in which they could be used to support curriculum teaching.

We asked participants to work in small groups and gave each group objects to study and a series of questions to answer. All the discussions were taped and transcripts made of them.

The objects discussed in this book are

At Leighton House
A Victorian photo album with its original photographs
A 19th century cup and saucer transfer-printed with anti-slavery imagery
16th and 17th century Islamic and 19th century De Morgan tiles
Portraits

At the Museum of London
A Roman roof tile with animal prints on it
A Victorian silk shoe
A medieval leather shoe
A 17th century candle holder
Victorian building bricks with pictures of children from different cultures on them
An Edwardian cup and saucer
Suffragette ephemera including chain belt and a tea cup
Genre, narrative and landscape paintings

Many of the objects that could be handled were examined behind the scenes in the morning. The paintings and some of the objects were on permanent display and we discussed them in the afternoon in the galleries where they were on show.

We asked participants to work in small groups and asked them a series of questions, which were intended to guide their discussions. These were

- What were your first thoughts when you looked at the object? What did you notice about it?

- What would be your professional view of these objects? What do you know about them? How would you analyse them? What interests you about them?

- How would you interpret these objects? What angle would you choose to emphasise in a museum or gallery? What bits of your knowledge would you choose to use?

- What questions would you ask of these objects in order to encourage other people, in particular children, to look at them?

- What cross curricular themes could be developed from these objects?

It became clear that bringing together a group of people with a range of different interests and specialisms was enormously effective in developing cross curricular approaches. The discussions ranged far wider than the scope suggested by the questions. As the groups worked with the objects and images they were able to build on their different knowledge and skills to open doors for each other and suggest a range of approaches which no one person, however creative, would have come up with on their own. We felt that these outcomes fully justified the focus group aspect of our research.

Someone confirmed our approach saying *'people planning cross curricular work should get a group together and discuss all the possibilities'*.

23

One painting we looked at in the Museum of London was *'Embankment'* by John O'Connor. An art historian and a scientist looked at this painting. They discussed how they would draw students' attention to the golden section in the painting and to the composition, colour and realism, but they also discussed the ways in which it could be used to stimulate and support work on the industrial revolution, transport, science and technology.

> *This one is easier for me, as a scientist. There are boats. There is smoke. In the foreground is Somerset House. A lovely ordered scene. The Thames. All kinds of power and transport. I see smoke, pollution (a pink glow in the foggy air) but at the time they wouldn't have thought pollution, they would have thought 'How wonderful, power'. You are very aware of the siting of the big railway station against the sky. It is almost like a Canaletto painted from the same spot. You could make a comparison between them.*

In the same museum, we also looked at a Roman tile with paw prints of some kind on it. Most museums, which have Roman tiles, will have something similar. An archaeologist and an art educator who is also a practising artist discussed it. The archaeologist talked about

John O'Connor, *The Embankment*, 1874, oil on canvas. Standing in front of this painting, a scientist and an art historian showed how different subject specialists can open up discussion about a painting.
(The Museum of London)

This Roman tile with a dog's paw prints on it quickly grabs the imagination of teachers and students alike. Dozens of objects in every local museum can provide starting points that are just as interesting, as our focus groups show. (The Museum of London)

how the tile was made and showed us the straw marks on the back where it was laid to dry. From looking at the construction of the roof tile and how it would be laid on the roof discussion moved on to creating a story to explain the paw prints and then on to music and drama

The movement of the animal, rhythm, an innate kind of rhythm over time, it naturally leads to music, to a series of punctuations. You could write a wonderful piece of music based on the rhythm of the animal's movements. You would take into account form, style, mood, rhythm, just as you would in the visual arts.

What became clear from all the discussions was the range of themes which can emerge from discussing objects and images. These themes had not been planned in advance. Rather, they emerged from the discussions that took place around the collections. They conclusively demonstrated the huge scope of quite ordinary objects and the range of projects, which they can stimulate and support.

Some of the themes that emerged were:

26

Values
Realism and fantasy
Stories and narratives
Natural forms

Materials
Construction
Imitation and reproduction
Conservation
Collections – how they are formed, displayed and interpreted
Taste (good, bad, changing fashions)

Trade and communications
The industrial revolution
The grand tour
The role of women
Class, gender and race – how they are perceived, how they are portrayed, how things have changed and how they have not changed

Homes
Childhood and toys
Light
Heating
Work
Food
Storage
Clothes
Fashion

If such a range of themes can be developed from the small range of objects we used with our focus groups then a group of educators brainstorming in their local museum or gallery could probably find ways of using the collections to support all their curriculum teaching. Certainly, the case studies and the focus groups together demonstrate both the versatility of objects and their astonishing power to stimulate discussion, creativity and ideas.

The case studies

The purpose of the case studies is to suggest ideas which educators can develop locally for themselves.

We wanted this book to include examples of real cross curricular projects. They would show how collections and exhibitions have been used by students of all ages and in a variety of ways and which had taken place in museums and galleries all over the United Kingdom. We looked for museums and galleries whose staff were prepared to spend time with us discussing their project and who could also provide access to some of the teachers who had attended the sessions so that we could discuss the visit with them too. We also wanted to find examples which had used objects and pictures that might be found in any local museum or gallery. The hope was that this would help to avoid some of the 're-inventing of the wheel' which goes on simply because everyone involved is too busy to write up details of the highly successful projects they run.

We advertised for possible case studies in a range of publications including GEM news, **engagements** and the *Museums Journal*. We wrote to Area Museum Councils, Regional Arts

Boards, County Museum Development Officers, Local Authority Arts Officers, Local Education Authority advisory staff and many others. We asked for details of any cross curricular projects they had been involved in or knew about.

We also went out and hunted for more. Once potential case studies had been selected, we then arranged to visit each gallery and museum to discuss the project both with the staff who had planned it and some of the educators who had used it. The interviews focused on:

How the project had been initiated and planned
Its aims
How the students had been prepared for their visit
The work done on site and in school
The short and long term benefits of the project for museum and gallery educators, teachers and students

The case studies in this book show how collections and exhibitions can be used to teach such things as history, art, English, French, geography, science, technology, music, drama and dance. They also look at some ways in which the projects might have been extended both on site and in the classroom. Every one of these projects exemplifies the importance of collaboration between museums, galleries and other agencies or specialists, such as artists, dancers and musicians. They could all be adapted by educators for use in their own local museums and galleries.

28

4

The case studies

ART AND DANCE

What happened?

A county museum officer for art and education was inspired to organise dance workshops for youth dance groups and adults. The one featured here involved PE and secondary school dance students. This was a direct response to an exhibition of paintings by the artist, Shirley Sully that was organised by Ithaca, the Oxford-based arts and disability organisation, held at Banbury Museum. The museum officer thought that some of the paintings of dancing couples *'were very expressive – angular features, blue, red and yellow faces – men in brightly coloured zoot suits, women in black – their movements appeared angular and threatening in some images and sensual, graceful, and sometimes pained, in others'*. He felt the work lent itself to interpretation through movement and dance, especially as it also showed *'figures stretching, squatting, crouching – sometimes ecstatic, sometimes in fear and pain'*.

How did it come about?

With help from the local council's dance officer, a dancer who had worked in a gallery before was identified. She would be able to help plan and deliver the workshops. The group also planned dance projects with youth dance groups and a workshop for local dancers and visual artists.

Who was it for?

Year 8, 9 and 10 students were the principal participants.

What was the point?

Many teachers of dance in school come from a PE background and the dancer felt that they generally approach the subject '*from a technical rather than a creative and educational point of view*'. Consequently, the workshops were structured to explore the kinetic energy of the paintings through discussion and guided, practical dance work. It was hoped, therefore, that **teachers** would find the workshop interesting for their own development. It would give **students** an opportunity to improve their interpretive skills in language and movement and help them to understand more about the art works by transforming their interpretations into dance.

The **dancer** wanted to introduce students and their teachers to an unfamiliar way of working, exploring the energy of the paintings rather than technique, yet building on the understanding of dance that they already possessed.

How did they prepare?

No preparatory material, apart from organisational details, was sent out to the schools in advance. The students were not prepared in any way, except that most of them had some experience of dance.

The teacher we interviewed felt that the novelty of the experience gave it greater impact. Few of the students had been to an art gallery before. In fact, the teacher was attracted by the spontaneity of the project '*If I'd had the information the term before, I wouldn't have done it*'. She was also attracted to the project by talking to the dancer who, she felt, '*sounded as though she knew what she was doing*'. It was an added bonus that transport to the gallery was offered free.

What did they look at?

A temporary exhibition of contemporary paintings open to the public during gallery hours.

What did the students do?

The museums officer got the students talking and developing a vocabulary to describe works of art. This made them aware of the similarities between the ways we talk about music and painting – such as colour, rhythm, movement, tone, and composition. The dancer re-introduced these words as starting points for interpretation through movement. Another exercise, designed to give the students a vocabulary for developing movements, also took place in the gallery. Standing in a circle they were asked to pass a movement on, much like the party game of Chinese whispers, so that the movement would change and take on new meaning as it journeyed round. Students were then asked to select a painting and to try to capture some aspect of it in movement.

The dancer wanted to move away from the idea of narrative and so emphasised that students should not merely imitate a pose. They should think about the kind of movements, which might go into making that shape. Individual responses were shown to the group in order to build up a vocabulary.

The afternoon session was held in a larger space where this repertoire of initial responses and actions could be developed into a performance. Here, working in pairs, the students made a selection of the movements they had seen articulated in the gallery and put them together, developing them in different ways. The dancer encouraged them to talk about the things they had noticed in Shirley Sully's work and to refer back to the paintings. The work done in pairs was shown in groups of six, thus providing interrelationships for yet further development and supplying most of the material for the end-of-day performance.

31

What did people learn?

The **teacher** felt that she had gained enormously from

Working with a professional dancer
Developing her ability to use different approaches to confidence and team-building
Taking ideas from paintings
Having been alerted to the potential of other such gallery events.

Taking the project further

In this case the workshop was not followed up in school as the students involved had come from different year groups. However, the teacher talked to those involved and it was clear that they all believed that they had benefited from working with a professional dancer. The students' participation had been voluntary, and the fact that two boys attended resulted in a dance module being offered to boys for the first time. Memories of an image from the exhibition have been used as the basis for a warm-up exercise for rugby.

32

Brainstorming for other ideas

In schools art, design and technology students could have been involved in a project like this. They could have

■ Designed and made sets for the dancers' performance piece
Made an installation for them to perform in
Designed and made masks, body ornaments and costumes for the dancers

■ Although paintings depicting moving figures inspired this art and dance project, visual art does not have to be about movement or dance to be suitable for exploration and interpretation in this way. Sculpture, since by its nature it is often to do with weight, balance, and three-dimensional relationships with space, is especially suitable for exploration through dance, as is expressionist, gestural and abstract work.

■ An art and design project could be developed through research into ways in which movement has been expressed through painting and sculpture – Futurism and Vorticism, for example.

- Dance students could make similar explorations and then their fellow students could draw the dance students from life then abstract from their work to make notation that the dancers then re-interpret
- Or students could take these notations into textiles, sculpture or ceramics
- Compose music in response to images which, in turn, could inspire more dance
- Make a documentary video about the working processes leading to a performance
- Work with a professional designer, musician or film-maker as Artist in School.
- Work could also be extended into language and literature. Students might describe the movements of the dancers and, using these appropriate words, perhaps translated into another language, write poetry or songs. They could look at poetry, which expresses movement such as Auden's *The Night Train* or Betjeman's *Jean Hunter Dunn*.

BACK TO THE FUTURE

What happened?

The Ulster Folk and Transport Museum education service has strong links with schools, advisory services and the Northern Ireland Education and Library Boards and has a tradition of collaborating with different education organisations. It should be noted that the Northern Ireland curriculum includes six statutory cross curricular themes. These are careers, economic awareness, health education, education technology, cultural heritage and education for mutual understanding.

This project was carefully constructed and practical science teachers were central to its development.

How did it come about?

The project was initiated and coordinated by the advisory teacher for education for mutual understanding (EMU) for the Southern Education and Library Board (SELB). SELB funded the project as an inter-board initiative that would be of benefit to schools across the province. This support was critical as it paid for cover so that teachers could be released to participate in team meetings. The EMU advisor liaised with science advisors and secondary head teachers to publicise the idea and seven teachers volunteered to participate. SELB also funded a resource pack that was distributed to every school in the province.

Who was it for?

The target audience was KS3 students studying cultural heritage and education for mutual understanding within the science curriculum.

What was the point?

The team's objectives reflected Northern Ireland's curriculum objectives. These include

- Students should be encouraged to express their ideas and respond to those of others

- Students should consider the benefits and drawbacks of applying scientific and technological ideas to themselves, industry, the environment and the community. They should begin to make personal decisions and judgements based on their scientific knowledge of issues concerning personal well being, safety in the community and care of the environment. They should begin to develop an understanding of how science shapes and influences the quality of their lives.

• Students should be given opportunities to develop their awareness of the role and importance of science in everyday life and how it is applied in a variety of contexts

How did they prepare?

The team spent three days at the open air museum working with the education officer to identify relevant themes. Once agreed, suitable sites and houses were selected for inclusion in the project and the team started work at the museum to collect information and generate ideas for activities.

Because some teachers commented that they would only consider using the project with older KS3 students who already had an understanding of basic scientific principles, preparatory work in this area was acknowledged to be essential prior to any visit.

35

On this basis, the team compiled a resource pack containing information about the activities that students would engage in and background materials, including photographs and drawings, from the museum archives. There were ideas for extension work in a range of subjects other than science, notably a role-play exercise and poetry.

What did they look at?

Buildings and sites re-erected in the grounds that concentrate on the social history of the area.

Overleaf: Science teachers formed part of the project team for *Back to the Future* which encouraged students to explore how science and technology have affected contemporary domestic life using buildings at the Ulster Folk and Transport Museum, County Down. Students can vividly contrast the life lived in the simple homestead, Meenagarragh (left) with the visible signs of affluence in the kitchen of the two-storey, slate roofed farm, Drumnahunshin, (right).

Harland and Wolff Photograph Collection, National Museums and Galleries of
Northern Ireland, The Ulster Folk and Transport Museum.

What did the students do?

The museum activities featured in the pack involved students in first hand study of buildings to explore how changes in science and technology have affected domestic life in the 20th century. Four main themes were explored:

1. *From thatch to tile*, compared construction materials in 1900 and the present day

2. *From matches to microwave* considered the development of materials used in domestic technology

3. *From potions to pills* focused on medical improvements and their influence on the quality of life

4. *From turf to turbine* explored advances in fuels used for domestic heating

Using the science-based methodology known as the jigsaw method students gathered information from the buildings and their contents and applied it to broader questions about the impact of scientific and technological change.

38

What did people learn?

The development of the project enabled the team of teachers and the museum educators to look at the collections in a new way. Working together ensured that the links made between collections and the science curriculum were valid and would meet the needs of **teachers** and **students.** It also made clear to the **museum education staff** that a social history collection can support other subjects.

The jigsaw technique was popular as it encouraged group interaction, fostered team building and promoted students' cooperative skills whilst at the same time enabling autonomy and responsibility for individual learning. In short, it provided opportunities to develop transferable skills.

Taking the project further

One teacher involved felt that the visit and the resource materials enabled him to introduce a wider range of teaching styles into his classroom teaching *'science teaching does not normally allow many opportunities for role-play, but working with historic buildings enabled my students to use drama to explore how science has changed lives'*.

This project reinforces the conclusions of our own focus groups. It demonstrates the value of team-work in pooling information and in generating ideas for activities.

Brainstorming for other ideas

Domestic life and the ways in which science and technology have changed it is a theme which can be explored in everyday ways that are accessible to students of differing abilities. Many social history museums have paintings in their collections that could add another dimension to looking at domestic life.

■ Students might explore upstairs/downstairs as represented in Victorian painting for example, and compare these representations with images of 20th century domestic life, perhaps in documentary photography. Students might then write *A day in the life of* ... Issues about idealisation, class, the place of women in society and attitudes to children could be raised. What skills do modern day cleaners need in comparison with the housemaid of the 19th century? How has 20th century imagery in advertising and packaging depicted domestic life? How has science and technology changed that imagery?

■ A photography project exploring different periods and styles of houses might lead to art and craft work in the construction of a street in clay or card. Art work might also include drawing domestic objects in different styles and contexts according to the imagined point of view of the retailer, the buyer, the user, second hand dealer, and so on. Students might study changes and the reasons for them in still life painting, looking at, for example, 17th century symbolism, Post Impressionism, Cubism, Dada and Pop art.

■ Using oral history as well as the exploration of attics and cupboards, students could develop their own exhibition about changes in technology, perhaps related to the kitchen. This might be called, *From wooden spoon to food processor.* It could pose such questions as 'Has

39

domestic life been improved?' or 'Who has benefited most from technology in the home? Wives and daughters or husbands and sons?' Alternatively, a debate could be set up to discuss 'What are the six most significant technological changes in the home this century?' and catalogue essays for the exhibition written as an outcome.

- Within a given budget students could design a bed-sitter for themselves which employs all the technology, imagined or real, they think necessary for their comfort and enjoyment. They could invent new technology for keeping the room clean and tidy.

- A visit to the Ideal Home exhibition or a study of magazines could lead to an illustrated essay on My Ideal Home.

BRAQUE

During a visit to the exhibition *Braque, the Late Work* at the Royal Academy students from the French Lycée in London were divided into two tours, one in English and one in French. These groups provided a stimulating and timely learning context for students with varied speaking, listening and writing skills in each language.

How did it come about?

A teacher booked a class visit to the exhibition. An education officer at the gallery grasped the opportunity for a bilingual approach to critical and contextual studies and arranged the tours.

Who was it for?

The project was for 31 KS2 students, some having English as their first language, but the majority French.

What was the point?

41

The **teacher**'s aims concerned art and culture, his area of responsibility in the school. In his words '*At school we don't open minds. It is important to see other things – part of our culture*'. He also believes that visiting galleries is a good way for his students to extend their vocabulary, especially that related to art and artists. However, the **education officer** also hoped to link to other curriculum areas in the course of the visit. These included

1. history, as Braque's late work was heavily influenced by WW2 and its shortages and restrictions,

2. maths, with respect to balance and proportion

3. music, with references to harmony and composition

She also wanted students to look, analyse, respond and develop speaking and listening skills during their tour. More specifically, she was keen to consider with them Braque's techniques and experimental working processes and the way in which he used similar imagery over a period of time.

42

Jeudi 6 mars, nous sommes allés voir *l'exposition Georges BRAQUE.*

Georges BRAQUE est né le 13 mars 1882 à Argenteuil-sur-Seine, près de Paris et il est mort en 1963.

En 1899, il copie son père en peignant des maisons. En 1908, il s'intéresse à Paul Cézanne qui lui montre dans ses peintures comment faire le cubisme.

BRAQUE se servait de beaucoup de textures dans ses tableaux. Par example, quand le tableau est encore mouillé, il y rajoutait du sable, de la cendre et même du tabac.

Nous avons vu une série de tableaux qui réprésentaient le studio du peintre avec ses peintures. Pour donner un sens de l'espace, Braque peignait des oiseaux en plein vol qui étaient parfois dissimulés. Il aimait se servir d'une association d'idées. Par example, une palette est un violon ou une guitare.

Nous avons aussi vu deux peintures représentant des tables de billiard avec des boules rouges et blanches. Il y en avait une qui était transparente, ce qui permet de voir les meubles derrière la table plus facilement. Braque faisait souvent revenir les mêmes thèmes dans un tableau en répétant les mêmes formes dans ou sur certains objets.

Il y avait aussi deux peintures d'oiseaux qui rentraient dans une boule noire avec en dessous un oiseau blanc qui faisait contraste avec le noir.

Le tableau qui m'a le plus impressionné était celui avec des tournesols, inspiré par Van Gogh.

Natasha ROSS – 7°5

On Thursday 6 March we went to see the exhibition *Georges Braque*

Georges Braque was born on the 13 March 1882 at Argenteuil-sur-Seine, near Paris, and he died in 1963.

In 1899 he followed his father as a house-painter. In 1908, he became interested in Paul Cézanne, who showed him through his paintings, how to make cubism.

Braque used many textures in his paintings. For example, when the painting was still wet, he would add sand, cinders and even tobacco.

We saw a series of pictures depicting the painter's studio with his pictures. To give a sense of space, Braque painted birds in full flight which were sometimes hidden. He liked to use associations of ideas. For example, a palette is a violin or a guitar.

We also saw two paintings of billiard tables with red and white balls. There was one which was transparent, which allowed us to see the furniture behind the table more easily. Braque often reused the same themes in a painting by repeating the same forms in or on certain objects.

There were also two paintings of birds which were forming in a black circle. With, below, a white bird making a contrast with the black ones.

The painting I remember the best was the one with sunflowers inspired by Van Gogh.

An English speaking student at the French Lycée in London wrote a review for her school magazine after visiting the exhibition 'Braque, the late work' at the Royal Academy, London.

How did they prepare?

Students were already familiar with galleries as they had made visits to see the work of Seurat, Giacometti and Mondrian.

The gallery education officer prepared the tours for this particular school around a schools' programme that was already in place for the exhibition.

The teacher went to a teachers' evening where packs about the exhibition were given out. These included background information, a junior guide called *Beginners' Braque*, a guide for secondary students called *Browsing through Braque* and ideas for follow-up in school. A colleague at the school translated the junior guide into French. Before the visit the teacher talked to students about the way an artist's work progresses through series of paintings and how Braque's work was a form of exploration and experimentation.

What did they look at?

Braque, the Late Works was a temporary exhibition. The paintings were primarily still life and interiors.

43

What did the students do?

The gallery education officer, who led the English speaking tour, encouraged students to use language creatively to describe aspects of the paintings. The tour started with photographs showing Braque in his living and working environment in the 1940s. She gave students some art historical and historical background to the exhibition. Then they looked at Braque's paintings linked by references to Cubism and diverse viewpoints, musical echoes, colour contrasts, use of space, foreground and background ambiguities, the significance of still life objects and the poetry of bird forms. The information she conveyed and their own analysis of the paintings gave the students a rich fund of knowledge and understanding for their work back in school.

After the tour, the students were given time to explore the exhibition on their own and to look at works they were particularly interested in. Teachers were encouraged to plan this into their day's timetable.

What did people learn?

Both **students** and **teachers** learnt how to make the most of a gallery visit. During it they considered:

Braque's way of working

The way in which he organised his paintings

How to look carefully at art works

How to talk about them, using appropriate vocabulary in a foreign language

How to articulate responses to colour and composition and mood

Taking the project further

Members of the class compared the two different tours and talked about the paintings they had seen. Then they wrote a review of the exhibition in French for their school magazine. The teacher intervened only in matters of spelling and French grammar, so that reviews were personal in their emphasis and direction.

Follow up work was also extended into practical art based on Braque's bird paintings. Reminders for this were provided in the form of postcards bought at the gallery. The students produced simple bird form paintings using only two colours. They were asked to remember their poetic responses to the recurring flying bird forms in Braque's late works. The students also reinterpreted their favourite work from memory, thinking about aspects of it that had been discussed at the gallery.

Brainstorming for other ideas

Since modern languages are not taught in isolation these days and should be put into a cultural context, often with an emphasis on literature, this case study shows how the term 'context' can be broadened out to include gallery and museum visits. It is not difficult to find paintings, sculpture and decorative arts made in France, Spain, Italy or Germany.

■ Exhibitions of work by non-western artists would be a rich resource for critical and contextual studies and language development, especially for those with English as a second language.

■ As we have seen, Braque's work was viewed in the context of the Second World War. Students might look at the subject of war through the work of artists such as Käthe Kollwitz and Otto Dix (both German); the photographer Cartier Bresson or the contemporary artist Christian Boltanski (France); Goya or Picasso's *Guernica* (Spain).

■ Students looked at still life painting in the Braque exhibition. It offers interesting subjects for vocabulary development, naming and describing the objects depicted.

■ Equally, looking at portraits might be used to develop vocabulary in relation to body parts, dress and character. Students might be asked

What do Ingres' portraits tell us about 19th century French society?
Do Degas' or Toulouse Lautrec's paintings tell us something different about it?

■ Contemporary work, especially sculpture, frequently invites a listing of the materials, found objects and processes involved in their making.

■ A level or GCSE students might like to prepare worksheets or write reviews of exhibitions in a modern language to be used by younger students in the school.

45

■ Art and design students could make an exhibition of their own work related to their study of European artists with labels written in the appropriate language. They could take a theme, such as the circus, carnival or the theatre and research how European artists have depicted it. Another theme might be Expressionism, Romanticism or Classicism.

CASTING SHADOWS

What happened?

This was a five-day Artists in School project in which visual artists worked with a storyteller. It included an INSET session for all the staff in the school and concluded with an exhibition of the students' work, entitled *Casting Shadows*, in the their local gallery, the Café Gallery in Southwark.

How did it come about?

Two visual artists initiated this project. They wanted to work with Year 3 and 4 students to explore the visual qualities and personal and cultural significance of everyday objects used in cooking and eating. They approached schools with their ideas and devised the project to meet the needs and interests of students in consultation with staff. They worked with a storyteller to develop the concept and raised funding for it.

Who was it for?

46

The target participants were to be eight and nine year old students. The art coordinator in the school we visited selected eight students from each of three classes to work directly with the artists to develop the project because they had shown a particular interest in the project and had some aptitude in art. The teacher also thought that they would benefit from the project. Most of them spoke English as a second language and some had special needs and behavioural problems.

What was the point?

The two artists wanted the students to '*produce work reflecting the differing significance of objects*'. **The Jamaican storyteller** wanted to draw out narratives from the students that would influence the appearance of the objects they were to make. **The teacher** we interviewed realised the value of Artists in School and thought that the project would enhance his students' drawing and making skills. He also felt that there would be other, intangible, benefits such as increased self esteem. He felt that it was important that students saw artists working locally as real and professional people. He also felt that involvement in such a project would benefit the reputation of the school.

Primary school students' work for *Casting Shadows* looks magnificent shown in a professional display at the nearby Café Gallery in Southwark, South London.

47

© Dave Allen

What did they look at?

At first it was intended that objects would be borrowed from a museum. However, this proved impossible and the project was resourced from the artists' and storyteller's own collections of domestic items. A cooking pot belonging to the storyteller's grandmother was particularly significant.

How did they prepare?

Early preparation had involved several meetings between teachers and the artists to plan the sessions in school. The INSET session showed teachers several different 3-D techniques using everyday materials such as paper and card. During the session they also made collages focusing on tone and shape and slides using coloured gels for projection. They were introduced to the ideas behind the project.

The project we examined began with introductory sessions for all the Year 3 and 4 students in the school in which the artists showed slides of their work and that of other artists interested in still life. These included Braque, Morandi and Richard Wentworth. The students were already accustomed to reading visual and written material projected by an epidioscope.

During the introductory day the storyteller worked with each class telling them the story of her Jamaican grandmother's cooking pot. Discussion followed about cooking in different cultures, the significance of meals as nourishment and nurture, different cooking utensils and imaginary meals and recipes.

What did the students do?

The remainder of the artists' five days in the school was spent working intensively with the 24 selected students. They made observational drawings of domestic containers and tools. They 'drew' with scissors and experimented with the shapes they made to make collages and slides for projection. The artists wanted to foster an understanding of tone, light, shadows and shade, form and volume, composing and framing, spatial relationships and positive and negative space.

They played imaginative 'games', such as 'What good things would you put in this container?' They invented additions to, and additional uses for, the objects they drew and made. Sometimes they worked in pairs so that they could talk to each other about what they were making and the stories behind them and they also told the artists about what they were doing and why. They made sculptural objects from cardboard and papier maché, which they decorated and embellished according to the stories they invented about them. They made up a past history for these objects, as if they had been discovered by an archaeologist, and the artists helped them to make their surfaces look like metal.

What did people learn?

The **class teacher** thought that the project gained prestige and excitement throughout the year groups. He thought that the Jamaican storyteller gave an extra dimension to the project while the **selected groups** also gained in terms of their artistic skills.

> 'In the morning we did stories with Dimela. And then we did collage with Sineid. I learnt that you can use positives and negatives ... Today we made containers. I learnt you can make 3D shapes with 2D paper ... I enjoyed it'? (Methela)

Students clearly felt proud that they had been chosen '*It is exciting when you have been chosen to work with real artists*' (Nathan). The fact that their work was professionally displayed in a local gallery was enormously appreciated. In the words of one student '*I like the pictures on the wall and I like this gallery and my work is lovely in this gallery*'. (Busola).

Speaking, listening and story making skills were developed throughout the project and contributed to a marked increase in self esteem.

Taking the project further

Together with work from another school participating in the project, examples of the students' work were displayed in an exhibition called *Casting Shadows.* The artists took care to display the work in an imaginative way surprising visitors by creating shadows, using the objects they had made, and projecting images. Students were invited to a celebratory viewing with their parents or carers.

49

One of the special qualities of the project was that it was an Artists in Schools event which created extra interest and focus for students with special needs and behavioural problems. This is an element that other educators might like to build upon, perhaps in a longer Artists in Schools project, since it was of value to the whole school.

Brainstorming for other ideas

■ We have mentioned that some museums and galleries work with artists in their education programmes. *Casting Shadows* might well have included a visit to a museum to look at cooking pots and utensils from different times and countries and to think about the different foods cooked in them. Students could consider what they were made of and conjecture what kind of heat source would be used to cook the food. They might be asked

- What kinds of materials make containers watertight? Heatproof? Easy to carry? Durable? Easy to clean? Easy to decorate?

- How was the food produced and processed?

- Where did it come from?

- What do we know about it in this country today?

- Where does our food come from?

- How do we prepare various foods?

■ Parents or grandparents might come into school and talk about food preparation and cooking, past and present.

■ The Jamaican Grandmother's Cooking Pot might lead to the question 'What kind of cooking pot did *my* mother's grandmother use?'

■ Having invented stories about the containers they were making for *Casting Shadows* students could have incorporated a narrative on to their object. They could have visited a museum to look at Greek or Wedgwood pots and then explored various ways of telling stories visually – hieroglyphics, story boards, strip cartoons and so on.

■ The use of papier maché and collage could have led to an exploration of the properties of paper. In what other ways can we make paper strong? How is it made? Or, historically, what things did the Victorians make out of papier maché?

■ The project might have included a study of ways in which women have been represented in domestic situations in paintings or in books about childhood experiences. (Authors like Bucchi Emmechetta, Cameron Sage, Maya Angelou, Adeline Yen Mah, Tony Morrison). How do these compare with the students' own experiences?

■ *Casting Shadows* touched on still life painting and introduced students and teachers to the work of 20th century artists. This could have been pursued in modern collections, but a visit to a historical collection to look at symbolism and narrative in still life could have developed the theme.

■ Since the exhibition at the gallery was arranged to cast shadows and dramatise the objects the students had made, the project might have included a study of shadow puppets from different cultures linking them to festivals, food and cooking pots.

51

GREEK VASE

What happened?

This was part of a pioneering summer literacy project run by a secondary school. It demonstrated the value of museum visits, working away from the classroom and the development of literacy skills through a cross curricular approach. It was delivered in a way that was completely new to the students.

How did it come about?

Having very little time to set up their summer literacy 'Flying Start' course, the head teacher rang the education officer at The Potteries Museum and Art Gallery, Stoke-on-Trent, and asked her what they had to offer on the chosen theme of Journeys. The education officer said '*The grand tour, the 18th century passion for travel and the objects they found, filched and brought back to England provided me with the idea for a project based on the journey of a Greek vase*'. The head teacher was attracted because '*the enthusiasm in her voice said that we would be on the same wavelength*'.

Who was it for?

The 37 students involved came from a cross-section of feeder primary schools and included three statemented students and one who had been excluded from primary school. The project took place in the holiday prior to their induction into secondary school.

What was the point?

The **head teacher**'s principal aim was to deliver extra literacy work in a fresh and exciting way. The **education officer** aimed to '*get a response from a different approach – to reverse what they* (the students) *would normally experience – not to start with words but to start with the objects and looking and then get to the words, putting them into context*'. She did not want to start with a literacy problem but with '*Somebody enthusing. To excite them – not a teacherly, but a story-telling approach*'.

One student's story written during the *Greek Vase* summer literacy project. Following their visit to the Potteries Museum, students word processed their stories and illustrated them with computer-generated images.

THE GREEK VASE

My name is Lord Edward Prince. I'm 30 years old ,I am a bit wrinkly.
I'm visiting most of the countries in Europe because I am going to go to Italy to unveil the Greek vase out of the earth.I'm a wealthy man ,I've came from England.
I've come to see the vase, I'm not married. The first country I'm visiting is France.
I really want to buy the vase and some pictures.
It's going to take me about two years , I have to go on a ship from England to France.
The road was very boompy and the wheel came of the chart . Then I had to go on horse pack .The vase is in Naples . I'm going to live in a hut for two or three days.
I was diging and I unviled the vase I was very happy it took me that long to get there.

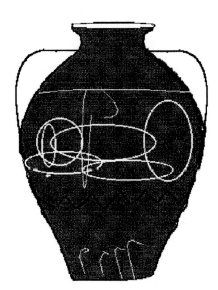

53

What did they look at?

The ceramics gallery was the principal collection used. Here the students were introduced to 18th century English pots, particularly those made by Wedgwood, which were inspired by the grand tour, classical Greece and archaeological finds made at this time. Students also looked at two ancient Greek pots from the museum's store.

How did they prepare?

The visit took place five days into the Flying Start course. Students were prepared '*minimally*' for the visit. They knew they were going to visit the museum, see a Greek vase and meet someone new. It was not thought necessary to give teachers preparatory materials. None of the group had visited the museum before, and the school did not use it on a regular basis, so all involved were coming fresh to the project. It goes without saying that the education officer prepared in detail for the visit.

What did the students do?

54

The visit began with a tour of the ceramics gallery. The education officer talked about pots that had been made locally for generations. She then brought out the two Greek vases from the store. She explained when and why they had been made and drew attention to their shape and decoration. She explained why they were damaged and where and when they had been found. Throughout the session she invited interaction in the form of comments and questions and related discussion to the students' own experience. She then told the group about the 18th century notion of the grand tour and the passion for classical Greece that overtook Europe. Time was spent talking about how wealthy aristocrats wanted to return to England with archaeological finds. Their passion formed the basis of the *Journey of the Greek Vase*.

The education officer then allocated students names and fictional characters from the European countries visited en route to southern Italy, where one of the Greek vases they had seen was discovered. These characters ranged from aristocrats to servants, shop keepers, inn keepers and archaeologists. In their assumed roles students talked about the countries they had travelled through en route to Italy, inns or buildings where they might have stayed, methods of transport used and the ways in which travellers recorded their experiences.

Students also made drawings of the Greek vase and of Wedgwood pots. Before they left the museum students were given flash cards to help them write down their story of the Greek vase. These listed the kind of place where travellers might have stayed, modes of transport, names of countries, and so on.

> 'Of course, these could be extended, but the idea was that the children would work in groups and cut off the cards to match the story they wished to write (back in school). They would write about the quest for the pot from the standpoint of the character they had been given (at the museum)'.

What did people learn?

The education officer thought that the **students'** speaking and listening skills had improved. They had been encouraged to use empathy in imagining the grand tour as a participant. **Teachers** felt that the students had developed their literacy skills and, in the process, had dipped into history, geography, technology and art. The students used computers to write up and illustrate their stories. They had also learnt something of the hierarchical structures in the 18th century. Significantly, they had learnt concentration, the importance of careful and detailed study and they had improved their questioning skills. Above all, the **head teacher** said that they had gained in confidence and she and they had discovered that the museum was an exciting and interesting place.

55

PGCE students, who accompanied the visit, were equally enthusiastic and a history teacher in her first year of teaching persuaded her colleagues that museum visits should be built in to schemes of work.

Taking the project further

Following *Greek Vase* the head teacher gave a number of presentations to secondary heads and cluster meetings of primary colleagues in which the role of the museum in the summer literacy project was explained. Consequently, further summer literacy projects have taken place in the museum.

Brainstorming for other ideas

■ Each of the themes that the education officer touched on – the grand tour, European geography, classical Greece, 18th century ceramics, the invention of 18th century characters – could have been developed as individual topics.

■ The invention of characters on the grand tour could be developed into drama and might include an examination of 18th century portraits and figure paintings. A speaking vase might have told its story of the journey from classical Greece to Roman Italy and a museum collection in Stoke on Trent.

■ This journey also suggests a debate, which could be formally researched and organised, about the appropriation of objects such as classical sculpture and ceremonial objects, (totem poles, shrunken heads and mummies for example) now housed in our museums and stately homes.

■ Since one of the vases used in our case study was made for ceremonial purposes, a development could have taken the form of an examination of vases and containers made for ceremonial and religious purposes in other places and times. This could easily involve a journey round a local museum. What vessels – cups, bowls and so on – are used for ceremonial or religious purposes today?

  • Can we invent one and make it?

  • What stories about our life and times would we put on a vase today?

  • Where else might these stories be told (verbally and visually) for future generations to find?

■ 18th century travellers had a certain vision of the grand tour. What picture do we have of travelling in European countries such as France, Italy and Greece today? Students might like to look at holiday brochures, advertisements, and documentary photographs in newspapers and magazines and compare them with 18th and 19th century paintings.

■ Classical influences on art and design might be explored in the local environment as well as in interiors, furniture, decorative arts and paintings. What is the golden section? Explore the ancient Greeks' use of mathematics in matters of proportion and beauty.

IN TOUCH WITH THE PAST

What happened?

This case study looks at an approach to exhibition planning that has been developed by Tweeddale Museum in Peebles to ensure that exhibitions can provide opportunities for cross curricular teaching and learning.

The exhibition was designed to provide hands-on opportunities for discovery learning. It provides a model for finding ways of challenging and livening up traditional museum displays and for consulting with teachers at the planning and evaluation stages.

How did it come about?

The museum initiated the project as part of its on-going policy of providing exhibitions that offer opportunities for cross curriculum learning and teaching. It is its policy to provide one exhibition a year to support the needs of local schools within the framework of the 5 to 14 Scottish National Curriculum.

57

Who was it for?

The project had two main target audiences, primary schools and special needs primary and secondary schools studying the 5 to 14 environmental studies and expressive arts curricula. In addition, a programme of weekly activities was offered to the local community.

What was the point?

The activities that accompanied the exhibition were designed to stimulate students to dip in to a number of additional subject areas: English, maths, science and technology.

How did they prepare?

Museum education staff worked with teachers over about 12 months to plan, design and evaluate problem solving work stations for visiting school groups.

What did they look at?

A touring exhibition entitled *In Touch with the Past* formed the basis of the exhibition. This was supplemented with archaeological material from the museum's own collection.

The museum arranged optional visits to local prehistoric sites.

What did the students do?

Two linked class sessions were provided for schools at the museum. In the morning the first session began with group orientation which took the classes through a simple introduction to archaeological methodology. Museum staff guided students round the exhibition where they could use five work stations that supplemented the displays. This gave the teachers a chance to stand back and observe the students at work. In Session 2 in the afternoon students could stay for craft and design activities.

Session 1 provided a range of problem solving activities to help students investigate the lives of early people, with an emphasis on craft and technology. The workstations touched on a number of subject areas including environmental studies (science, social subjects and technology), English language (listening, writing, reading and talking) and mathematics (problem solving, enquiry, shape, position and movement). The activities were

Station 1, An introduction for the whole class, looking at landscape and archaeological methods.

1. sort a variety of landscapes into those that showed signs of early habitation and those that did not.

2. consider what features would have encouraged early people to choose to live there

For the next three stations, the students, working in groups were required to

Station 2, Home, food and shelter.

1. consider how different shelters would have been constructed and food found in different environments

2. consider the tools and materials that might have been used

Station 3, Hunting.

1. consider the reasons for hunting animals, the methods used and the tools available to early people.

2. consider what uses could be made of the animals they caught

3. try out scraping skins with flints

Station 4. Toolmaking (stone)

1. compare tools of different materials and use a sequencing exercise to help place them in chronological order.

2. look at flint knapping and identify the special properties of flint and the kinds of tools that were made from it

Station 5. Toolmaking (metal) This was only used with older students who were required to

1. explore the impact of metal technology on tool making

2. look at how heat and fire changed early technologies

In the second session students took part in practical art and craft activities. Teachers chose from a menu of activities including working with clay, cave painting, drama, making plaster casts of prehistoric axe heads and other tools, dyeing, basket and textile weaving. All this took place in a prehistoric 'scene set' gallery.

59

What did people learn?

The **students** gained from the hands-on activities that developed their enquiry skills and an interest in a variety of subject areas. The sessions with the craftspeople helped to raise awareness of how skilled early man was and how their crafts have been adapted for use today. **Teachers** appreciated that a museum visit, together with a specially constructed exhibition and related activities, could stimulate a range of classroom activities which they could develop to meet their own curriculum targets.

Brainstorming for other ideas

■ Following their investigations into the lives of early people, students could explore their school grounds, local park or surrounding countryside in terms of what is there to enable them to survive in that locality without the benefit of conventional support. How would they make a shelter? Containers for food and drink? What would they eat? What would they wear? How would they cook? Would they need to cook? Small groups might be given a specific area as 'their' country and encouraged to barter with other groups for materials or sustenance not found in their country.

■ Having looked at early myths and festivals students might be asked the following questions: Who is the god/goddess of your country? What kind of ritual would your god/goddess respond to? What kind of objects would you need to make? What kind of performance would you need to make?

■ Problems (wars) might develop between the different countries about boundaries, pathways, access, water supplies and so on. How are they going to be solved through diplomacy and conference?

■ A display might be made to tell future archaeologists about the way of life they have invented and the objects they make and use. Comparisons could be made between these 'prehistoric' objects and technologies and the ones they use at home.

■ Students might learn about what was going on in the rest of the world with regard to craft and technology when Stone Age man was active in Europe.

■ A study of the media, film and books could reveal how Stone Age man has been represented in our century. Does this representation tie up with what was learned in the museum? An artist or craftsperson in school could show how to make shelters, containers or images from natural materials.

■ Cave painting might stimulate thoughts about the most powerful images of our day (media and advertising?). How would these be interpreted by future generations? How would a stone age person see our world? What would impress him or her about the things we make and use? What would they think was the most useful? Students might imagine they are this person and write about contemporary objects as if they had never seen them before.

SPLASH!

What happened?

Splash! was shown within the context of another interactive display, '*Something Borrowed, Something Blue*' and an installation, '*Vertical River*' by contemporary artist, Tom Hackett. The theme of Water had been chosen as the museum's contribution to 'Gallery Week'. This annual national initiative that began by highlighting education work in galleries has since expanded to include work in museums too and in 2000 was known as Museums and Galleries Month.

Splash! was the name of both a project and an exhibition by and for three to five year olds from a local nursery school. The *Splash!* exhibition featured paintings on the theme of water that the children chose from the museum's permanent collection. Alongside the paintings the museum displayed interpretive work that the children made in response to the original works of art.

How did it come about?

61

The gallery and exhibitions officer and an experienced nursery teacher, who would lead the workshops, devised the *Splash!* project to expand and promote workshops that had previously been organised on a one-off basis for small groups of very young visitors to the gallery. They wanted to raise the profile of the museum's nursery workshops with other visitors.

Who was it for?

Apart from the nursery school children who took part in the *Splash!* project and the children who attended exhibition workshops, a more general adult audience was expected for the exhibition. It was intended to inform them about the perceptions of very young children when faced with complex and challenging works of art.

© John W. Rogers

Under 5s in Worcester thought it would be fun to make their own interpretation of A.N. Pybus's print, *Bondi Beach.* To make it really interactive, they wanted other children visiting their exhibition, *Splash!,* to be able to add their own decorated patches as well.

62

What was the point?

The gallery and exhibitions officer and the **nursery teacher** wanted to work intensively with a group of three to five year olds. The overall intention was to provide the children with '*the very best experience*'. They saw the project as a training opportunity for nursery teachers and parents in best practice approaches to museum and gallery education for young children. In addition, it was hoped that a young child's point of view would make the **general visitor** see with new eyes. For the **children**, the project also served as a focus for a wide-ranging investigation around the theme of water. The project offered learning opportunities in art, English, science and technology.

What did they look at?

A selection of paintings and prints from the museum's collection that were connected to the theme of water. These included '*David's Pool*' by Howard Hodgkin and '*Bondi Beach*' by A.N. Pybus as well as works by Julius Olsen and Stanhope Forbes.

How did they prepare?

1. *Training for staff and parents.* The workshop leader led a training session for teachers that supported the programme of INSET organised by the local nursery school. Parents were also shown suitable approaches to art education for very young children. Another training session was organised for gallery and museum staff to ensure that '*everyone was pulling in the same direction*'.

2. *Project work on water.* The children investigated the different properties of water and the ways in which it is encountered and used in everyday life. The seaside was deliberately avoided in an effort to concentrate on aspects of water that the children could experience for themselves. This included thinking about the bath, and about washing themselves and their clothes, and even washing cars – a visit to a car wash and a picnic by the river formed part of this preliminary phase. Other work included language, poetry and stories, science, movement, drama, songs and music in addition to art and technology. Children considered transparency and reflection, sinking and floating and other qualities of water, all of which made them very aware of the medium before they made their contributions to the Splash! exhibition. During this time, prints that could be related to the theme of water from the gallery's print loan collection were taken to the nursery school and the children also visited the gallery.

What did the children do?

They made a rich range of interpretive work in different media. They decided, for example, to make their version of Pybus' *Bondi Beach* as a wall hanging. They used fabric paints, pens, sponge painting, hand- and mono-prints to create the various elements of the hanging. They thought it would be fun to be able to change the picture by moving the people, fish and boats around. They also thought that other children visiting the exhibition could then add their own decorated patch to the hanging. These ideas were realised using Velcro patches. The original *Bondi Beach* was 'improved' by adding fishing boats, a lighthouse and sea monsters.

The children also made 'dip and dye' pictures inspired by Howard Hodgkin's print, *David's Pool*. They used squares of unbleached, re-cycled kitchen paper, which they folded, twisted and dipped into trays of vegetable food colouring.

Language use was stimulated by other imaginative exercises around the water theme. The workshop leader explained '*We sprayed water on the stems of bronze fennel and dropped it on to hosta leaves to allow the children to compare water droplets with a diamond necklace. In fact, throughout the whole project there was more talking and looking than making*'. She collected children's verbal responses to the paintings and prints and used these as the basis for interpretative labels, interactive exhibits and activity sheets for the *Splash!* exhibition.

What did people learn?

The children's work was truly cross curricular. The value of museum and gallery visits in developing literacy in young children was clearly recognised '*there ... you are bringing in different words all the time. I think that's an important part. You go into a museum or art gallery and some of the words you use are words that children have never heard before ...you may be using a word they have heard before but in a different way, and I think that's quite exciting*'.

Equally important was the children's development of personal and social skills – the self esteem resulting from the pleasure and pride of helping to put together an exhibition. They learnt to experiment and think for themselves. As the nursery head teacher said '*children should have the time and space to be able to develop, expand upon or consolidate* [what they have been shown] *if they want to*'

Taking the project further

In other case studies we have outlined ways in which gallery and museum visits have been followed up in school. In this case, the follow-up consisted of other nursery school groups and families visiting the *Splash!* exhibition that the nursery school children had interpreted.

Brainstorming for other ideas

Splash! is an excellent example of the inventive use of the cross curricular potential of displays of paintings.

■ If educators wanted to explore other areas, they might consider looking at museum objects linked to water. For example, containers – kettles, teapots, jugs, buckets and so on.

■ Following this, they might look at maths and measurement. Which utensil holds the most? How many cups go into a jug? How many jugs go into a bucket?

■ Look at and discuss objects related to washing clothes, such as a mangle or a washboard. How and where did people wash clothes in the past? How do we wash clothes today?

■ Look at watery features in the local environment, such as drinking troughs, fountains, waterfalls, swimming pools, ponds ... What was, or is, their purpose? Who are they for?

■ Talk about and design together the ideal swimming pool. What do young people need? What do old people need? Should it be inside or outside?

■ Think about what we drink. Do we need water to make it? Why do we need to drink?

■ Find out about the kinds of creatures which live in or near water.

65

STRIKE A LIGHT

What happened?

Strike a Light was a teacher-led workshop which took place in the classroom at Tullie House Art Gallery and Museum, Carlisle, and formed a regular part of the education programme there. It was easily resourced from existing collections and could be applied to a range of class topics such as light, energy or colour.

How did it come about?

This hands-on workshop was developed by the museum's education officer in response to a number of approaches from local primary schools requesting activities and resources for KS1 students. The education staff therefore began to work on a number of ideas and consulted with teachers before they settled upon the programme.

Who was it for?

66

KS1 students were the target audience but the project proved to be adaptable for KS2 students as well.

What was the point?

The museum education staff wanted to create a workshop that would be teacher-led and therefore adaptable to the requirements of individual groups. It was developed to encourage young students to use and improve their observation and investigation skills by exploring how people at different periods in the past managed to light their homes. General skills in the use of objects were implicit in the workshop and questions about them were devised to encourage discussion and make the approach relevant to both history and science.

What did they look at?

The students looked at a handling collection of oil lamps, rush lights, candles and gas, paraffin and electric lights.

How did they prepare?

The museum staff consulted extensively with local teachers and devised a programme based around an initial session in the museum classroom. Teacher training and refresher sessions were organised. Teachers' notes were devised as support. A supplementary resource pack that teachers could buy was also developed in order to provide more in-depth information about the history of light and the science of light and colour. The teacher we interviewed had prepared her 2nd year infant class by discussing different lights and how people in the past had made light using the material and technology available to them at that time.

What did the students do?

The workshop in the museum classroom began with groups of students, each assisted by an adult helper or teacher, discussing a wide range of objects grouped according to the energy they used. To encourage discussion the adults were issued with a sheet of questions that focused attention on how the different lights were designed and how they worked. The questions were:

- What is it made from?
- How does it feel?
- Does it smell?
- What could it be used for?
- Is it a light? Where does the light come from?
- What makes the light? Is it fire or something else?
- If it is fire, what fuel does the lamp burn? Is It oil, gas, wax, animal fat or something else?
- If it is a light, is it an oil lamp, a rush light, a candle, a gas or paraffin light, or an electric light?
- If it is not fire, what form of energy makes the light?

These questions encouraged observation and deduction and were expressed in a way that would be equally successful for history or science topics.

Once each group had worked through their set of objects a plenary discussion enabled them to share their findings. Students also undertook three practical activities: dipping candles, rush peeling and an investigation of an electric circuit.

67

Strike A Light
Teacher's Notes

CARLISLE
CITY COUNCIL

You should allow 1¹/₂ - 2 hours for this lesson

This lesson has been structured for Key Stage 1 and 2 and can be easily adapted for your own class. The broad theme of the lesson is the history of light but it would complement any topic on light.

When You Arrive

On arrival please go to the Admissions Desk with your Booking Form and payment. The cost of this activity is £1.00 per child or 50p per child if your school is in the Tullie House User Group. This charge is to cover the cost of materials used in the lesson.

If your class need the toilet before the lesson we advise you to use the main ones near Reception.

You will then be met by one of the Education Staff who will take you to the Activities Room. There is space outside the room for coats and bags. There is a toilet at the end of the corridor which is also adapted for people with a disability.

In The Activities Room

Your class needs to be divided into 5 groups. You should have at least 1 adult assigned to each group. If you have a small class you can have fewer groups, but it is essential that you have 1 adult for every 6 children. It is preferable this does not include yourself so that you can supervise the whole session.

The room will be set out with 5 tables of objects and activities. Each table will have related objects and an activity, for example, on the Candle Table you will find different types of candles, holders and a candle making activity.

Please ensure that the children sit down, but do not touch anything, until you have talked to them about the correct way to handle objects (some of which are extremely fragile).

This is a typical briefing sheet for teachers. It was prepared by education staff at Tullie House, Carlisle for their project *Strike a Light* aimed at KS1 and KS2 students.

68

Suggested format of the session

Introduction by the Session Leader   **10 mins**

*   What is light? Where does it come from? Why do we need it?

*   Explain to the children that they will be looking at different kinds of lights and things associated with light. Most lamps consist of a container to hold some fuel and a wick, but the variations on this theme are numerous.

     Each table of objects is themed around a different type of lamp: oil, rush lights, candles, gas and paraffin, and electric. They should look at the objects carefully and see if they can work out what kind of lights they are looking at, how they worked and whether each object is old or quite new.

*   How to handle the objects, drawing particular attention to glass objects, the wax pot and the objects on the front bench which pupils cannot touch.
     1.   Always pick an object up with 2 hands
     2.   Never walk around the room with an object
     3.   Never stretch across the table to reach something
     4.   Don't force things: there are lots of bits to unscrew or open on these lamps, but of course they are very old and may not work as new

Object Handling and Activities   **1hr 15/30mins**

Each table will have a different theme and some also have an activity.
          Oil lamps
          Rush light and a rush peeling activity
          Candles and a candle dipping activity
          Gas and paraffin lamps
          Electric lamps, a circuit making activity and a giant optic fibre

Each table will be provided with a list of the lamps on that table, a sheet of questions that can be used by the adult with each group to guide the children, paper, pencils and crayons. You will find these notes included in this pack. The children will rotate around the 5 tables during the session.

Talk by the session leader about the objects which they have not been allowed touch   **5 mins**

69

What did people learn?

The **museum education staff** thought that the workshop sessions were successful because they helped students to engage directly with museum objects. They also helped the museum education service to demonstrate to schools the broad educational relevance of its collections.

The **teacher** we spoke to was very enthusiastic about the workshop. Apart from encouraging **students** to observe and investigate objects, it provided an opportunity for them to express their ideas and talk to each other about what they had found out. She welcomed the chance to make links across different subject areas and to help students make connections between broad, science concepts and real objects and to explore how science and technology is applied to everyday situations. She felt that a key strength of the programme was that it offered a complete package for teachers, providing all the materials and knowledge that they needed to teach the programme which they did not have time to research and develop for themselves.

70

Taking the project further

Both teacher and students liked the fact that there were things to take home from the workshop, including drawings and the candles that they had made. In school, students made a wall display of their drawings and made a collection of objects for their own class museum about lights and different sources of energy.

Initially, the workshop did not make links with other objects in the museum's collections and the classes did not visit the museum. However, because the half-day handling workshops proved so popular, the museum staff felt it would be appropriate to devise more materials and displays to supplement them so that teachers would feel confident to take their students into the museum if they wished.

One such addition was a worksheet on looking at light in the galleries where there was a prism display which could be used to demonstrate how light is made up from the colours of the spectrum.

Brainstorming for other ideas

■ Work on different colours of the spectrum and colour mixing might follow a visit. Experiments might lead to a comparison between students' colour mixing and the painting techniques of Pointillisme and Impressionism.

■ Students might also look at moods invoked by particular colours in paintings and write poems or stories in response. They might also look at the different ways in which colour is used in advertising and shop window displays. Paintings could also provide a focus for a study of light and dark (chiaroscuro) in the work of painters such as Caravaggio or Rembrandt. Wright of Derby's paintings of candle lit scientific experiments are particularly exciting.

■ Students will be surprised at the range of tone and tint they can achieve with black and one primary colour. Practical art work might also involve photographing a still life lit in different ways and from different angles. How do the colours and mood of the object change?

■ In science and technology students could look at the history of photography accompanied by practical activities such as photograms and pinhole cameras. Projects they might investigate could include

- Why do we need light?
- Why do plants need light?
- Why do we need to protect some things from light?

■ The symbolism attached to the sun, moon and stars is rich in art and literature. Students might explore the use of metaphor – the light at the end of the tunnel, a shining example, reaching for the moon.

■ Teachers might like to challenge the cliché that light is good, while dark (or black) is bad. Myths about light and dark, day and night might be studied in addition to festivals of light such as Divali. Why do some people light candles in church or on special altars on, for example, the Day of the Dead in Mexico?

■ During *Strike a Light* students looked at various forms of lighting. This work could be extended to a study of the design of electric lighting in the home, the street, the supermarket, and so on. How are lights designed for specific purposes? Who needs special lighting for their work?

■ At the museum students learned how an electric circuit works. Transparent coloured paper, plastic bottles and other translucent objects can be transformed into light sculptures using home-made circuits.

71

SWANSEA AT WAR

What happened?

This project was characterised by collaboration and development. It was a collaboration between education officers at the Maritime and Industrial Museum, the Glynn Vivian Art Gallery and the local education authority, and also used the collections at the City Museum. In addition, the bus bringing children to the project took a prepared route through the city.

In its second phase, a Theatre in Education company, Theatre West Glamorgan, entered the collaboration. Thus a project which started with a specific exhibition of paintings by Will Evans of the Blitz in the city as its main focus, developed into one in which, in its second year, a performance about evacuees, *It'll all be over by Christmas*, became central.

How did it come about?

The gallery's education officer started work on an idea related to the Will Evans exhibition. It became clear that, for the paintings to be set into an historical context, other collections and organisations needed to become involved.

Who was it for?

Key Stage 2 and 3 students studying social history connected to the Second World War within the Welsh national curriculum took part. A survey of teachers in the area had highlighted this as a popular programme of study, especially if it included a local history perspective. The project also related to the art curriculum and, in its second phase, to drama.

What was the point?

The **principal aim** of the project was to '*inform students on the nature and violence of the impact of the bombing of the town and the state of mind of the people here at the time ... to think about types of evidence we have for understanding the history of the time*'.

In addition, the **education officers** involved wanted students to '*learn through a series of quick experiences and from different resources*'. The **teacher** we spoke to, from a tiny village school just outside the city, was attracted to the project for his class of 20 Year 4, 5 and 6

Opposite: Will Evans' paintings of bomb damage in the centre of Swansea were the starting point for both the project Swansea at War and for the topic web shown on page 4.

students, not only because of its relevance to the history curriculum but because '*it has everything for children*'. It also built on his own personal interests and was angled towards the local scene.

How did they prepare?

In addition to using the collections at the museums, slides of work by internationally-known artists were borrowed from a national collection in order to enlarge students' perceptions about the ways in which individuals record war. '*... You don't have to be Will Evans to be a good artist. I didn't want 'Let's draw a Will Evans'.*'

The museum offered preparatory sessions for teachers and, in the second phase, an opportunity to see a preview of the play. Teachers were briefed about the organisation of their visit, things to point out on their bus tour of the city, slide talks, work in the gallery and the museums and about the performance of the play.

Teachers' notes were written as a guide and to offer help for the self-directed aspects of the day. The institutions involved produced two packs of resource materials for the schools to use as preparation and/or follow up.

What did they look at?

The Will Evans paintings which inspired the project

Objects connected to the war in the city: photographs and posters and objects from the handling collection such as gas masks

The city itself was used to provide evidence and develop the story.

What did the students do?

The students were offered a fund of interactive experiences related to World War Two which could be drawn together by their teacher back in school and which covered all aspects of the curriculum.

What did students learn?

They learned about '*the human side of war – how people remember and record it*' and the different styles and approaches that artists use to represent it. They learned about dramatic interpretations of war. The impact of the bombing of their town was brought home to them through maps and photographs. Through themed background information and images teachers were able to show them that their visit was about '*... Your history. Your past. The community around you. Change*'.

Taking the project further

The teacher we interviewed used the visit as the focus for a whole term's work touching on all areas of the curriculum. His topic work illustrates this (see page 4).

The Theatre in Education performance undoubtedly had an impact on his class, but its absence would not prevent the project from being run again using the permanent collections in the gallery and museums.

During the project the teacher added his own resources such as films and television programmes and encouraged local people, one of whom collected war memorabilia, to reminisce with the class.

77

Brainstorming other ideas

- A Second World War project does not have to take place in a town that sustained significant bomb damage, as in Swansea. Sources of material can include

  - Local museums' handling collections

  - Paintings in local galleries by artists like Paul Nash, C R Nevinson, John Piper and Henry Moore

  - Slides and postcards, perhaps from the Imperial War Museum or Regimental Museums

  - Television and film

- Topics to consider could also include fashion, food, changes in women's life, employment

- Comparisons might be made between

  - Visual representations of war at different times (for example, Greek relief sculpture, the Bayeux tapestry, Goya, Otto Dix, Lady Butler, Käthe Kollwitz and cartoons).

  - Images with poems and excerpts from novels.

  - Reminiscences from people who can remember the war with accounts in children's books

  - Newspaper reports of war in 1940 and nowadays

  - Is war about honour and glory or death and disaster?

- How have changes in medical knowledge and the physical and psychological damage of war affected our attitudes to it? How has technology changed warfare and attitudes to it? Work might extend to the movement of refugees and emigration, then and now.

THE EGYPTIANS

What happened?

The Egyptians was unusual because it was designed for secondary students to encourage them to take a fresh look at their local museum's Egyptian collection, which most of them had visited as primary school students.

How did it come about?

The art education officer at Bolton Museum and Art Gallery designed a half-day session in the Egyptian gallery, both to respond to a school's request, *'Could we do something with the Egyptians?'* and to fulfil a desire on her part *'to get underneath the skin of the Egyptian display'*.

Who was it for?

The workshop was designed for Year 10 students studying art, craft and design.

What was the point?

The art education officer wanted to provide opportunities for work in education for personal relationships, religious education and English. She wanted to focus on the meaning and function of the Egyptian artefacts. The workshop was intended to promote the Egyptian gallery in a new and exciting way, to use grave objects to reveal information about themselves and to enable students to think about their own identity by reflecting on what items they would like to take with them into the next world. **The art teacher** wanted her students to *'get the feel of the Egyptians and their art'* and to learn to use local collections as source material for their own work.

How did they prepare?

The art education officer and the teacher met to chat before the visit, and the students were told about the format for the session and what would be required of them. However, the teacher wanted them to come to the museum fresh, and did not want to influence them beforehand knowing that, once there, they would be stimulated and given plenty of ideas.

What did they look at?

The Egyptian room in the museum was the main focus for the project. In addition, students looked at slides of artworks by contemporary artist Susan Hiller.

What did the students do?

At the start of the session the students were introduced to the Egyptian room. They were encouraged to think about the very contrasting reasons for the designing and making of the objects long ago and for their current display. The art education officer pointed out, for example, that the hieroglyphics on the coffins were made as religious texts and spells to protect the dead person from evil spirits. They were not made as decorative objects to be displayed in a glass case.

The students were given a brief account of ancient Egyptian attitudes to death, memorials and the spirit world. They were told how mummified bodies were bandaged with linen and how, in the case of wealthy people, jewels and amulets were placed inside the bandages. Provision in tombs for the spiritual and magical needs of the dead person included amulets, texts, statuettes of gods, funerary boats, ushabti figures, tomb paintings and prayers and offerings. The dead person would also need the accoutrements of their earthly life.

Students were also introduced to Susan Hiller's work. She was originally an archaeologist who looked at grave objects in terms of their function rather than their aesthetic qualities. However, as an artist, she looks at these objects in a more subjective manner. The students were to be led in a similar way.

They were asked to draw objects that they found odd, confusing or interesting. They were warned that they would be asked to justify their choice. They reassembled to talk about what they had drawn and why, writing a list of related words that were put on a flip chart so that they had a word picture about the group's experience in the gallery.

They were asked to think again about objects having a spiritual value for the living and the dead and to consider objects in their possession, such as lucky charms or iconic images, which had special meaning and resonance for them – a preciousness which did not relate to monetary value. The art education officer suggested that they might like to make their own set of charms, jewels and amulets, perhaps weaving them into bandages. Or they might make pots or other precious containers decorated with meaningful marks. She ended with the idea that these objects should be of personal value that they would like to take with them to the next world.

What did people learn?

The **students** learnt to look beyond the surface quality of objects and understand that, in this case, the Egyptian artefacts were made for a very specific purpose, not for museum visitors to look at. They considered the different values that objects may have. They learnt to talk about and justify their personal responses to them and they developed an appropriate vocabulary.

Taking the project further

Back in school the students made sheets of decorated images and design ideas as reference for the wealth of 'precious' objects in a variety of media. These included scarabs, medallions and containers such as beaded boxes with shawabti inside, jewels tucked into bandages, jewelled collars, scrolls of handmade paper, masks with wire work, stitching and beadwork, silk paintings and lino cuts on gold and silver paper.

Brainstorming for other ideas

- Since primary students study the Egyptians and many museums have Egyptian collections, this is a project that might be developed by a secondary school working in collaboration with feeder schools. The objects that the secondary students made might form an exhibition for primary students to explore.

- The principle of linking artists and makers from antiquity with more modern ones could be followed up in more detail. Bridget Riley has made abstract work about Egypt, whilst 19th century artists, such as Alma Tadema, were fascinated by north African exotica.

- Research in local cemeteries, graveyards and churches might lead to discussion about Christian attitudes to death and the next world.

- What kind of people were tombs made for in this country?

- Why is death more of a taboo subject in contemporary culture than it was in the 19th century?

- Students could look at descriptions of death scenes in 19th century novels.

- How do 20th century British and Mexican attitudes to death contrast?

- Why do people have beliefs about life after death?

- What about Greek mythology?

- How can Greek myths be re-written using contemporary characters and ideas about the next world?

- How do the Egyptian grave objects compare with those made in ancient China? Who made the objects?

- Who are the living gods in our day and age?

■ Students might research and discuss style in art and design.

- Why did the Egyptians choose to stylise tomb art?

- How has Egyptian design influenced design in this country? Why was this influence particularly strong in the early 19th century and again with Art Deco in the 20th century?

- What is the 'official art' of our day?

■ The design and technology aspect of a project related to the Egyptians could be extended to a study of architecture and building methods.

■ Consider how new technology, such as X-ray and DNA testing, has made in-depth research into Egyptian mummies possible. How have other technologies influenced research methods?

■ Conventions of beauty might form another subject for comparison and discussion, perhaps using 20th century media imagery or the film Anthony and Cleopatra. How do notions of perfection change?

■ Since many museums hold Egyptian and other ancient collections from abroad, students might discuss the reasons for this. Were our forebears collectors or plunderers?

WHO'S BEEN FRAMED?

What happened?

This was a curriculum development project in which teachers visited the National Portrait Gallery (NPG), Montacute House and the Royal Albert Memorial Museum, Exeter, with a view to developing new schemes of work in history and art. Subsequent schoolwork was documented for a publication and an exhibition so that the participating teachers' ideas could be disseminated. As an INSET project it shows how collaboration, whether local or national, between gallery or museum staff and LEA advisory services bring together a stimulating mix of knowledge and skills and has an impact beyond the project itself.

How did it come about?

It was initiated by the NPG's education department and Devon curriculum advisors for history and art and developed as an outreach project for the NPG.

Who was it for?

It was intended for teachers from all sectors. In the event it involved seven secondary, one middle and 12 primary school teachers. The curriculum development project in the school we visited benefited 250 Year 8 and 9 mixed-ability students.

What was the point?

The aim was to explore the use of portraits in art and history and to give **teachers** direct access to original works. The intention was to show teachers in a practical way that there are crossovers between programmes of work in history and art which will not compromise the uniqueness of each subject. The **regional organisers** of *Who's Been Framed?* saw it as an opportunity to establish a way of working that could be developed in future and used as a resource for their advisory work.

How did they prepare?

An introductory meeting for everybody and local evening workshops introduced and supported the project. The NPG provided a pack, *Looking at Portraits*, and Devon Curriculum Advice produced a range of support materials. These were organised under headings such as 'The functions and uses of portraits' and 'What to look for in a portrait' and included notes on symbolism, the historical background to portrait painting and costume. There was also information about specific paintings. Ideas for art projects were included.

What did they look at?

They looked at 18th and 19th century portraits in the NPG collection, 16th and 17th century portraits, on loan from the NPG, at Montacute House, and the NPG touring exhibition of 20th century works including photographs. This exhibition, *The Room in View*, was showing at the Royal Albert Memorial Museum in Exeter.

What did the teachers do?

84

On their visits to the galleries the teachers worked with the advisors and NPG education staff analysing and interpreting the portraits. In the light of their visits they tried out art and history projects with their students and, as a result, developed new approaches to the curriculum.

The teacher we interviewed introduced students to the language of portraits. One project was to '*produce portraits of 20th century personalities whose lives, work and achievements have some connection with Tudor personalities. In constructing their own portraits of the religious, the royal and the romantic, the heroic, the famous and the infamous, students were asked to consider and experiment with the artistic techniques introduced to them during the course of the project*'.

What did people learn?

The history teacher we interviewed thought that the project had raised the profile of art and history in the school and it had made a profound impact on her own teaching. She had developed new schemes of work and had been encouraged to look at cross curricular links, which had had an immediate and noticeable impact on her students.

Opposite: This is just one example of the support material for teachers produced by the team working on the education project *Who's Been Framed?*

How do we understand the Messages contained in the Portrait?

Portraits need to be 'decoded'. Artists use various techniques, some of which are particular to a period or painter, to give information. Tudor artists used several methods to send messages in their portraits. Colours, clothes, expressions, poses, backgrounds and accessories often had symbolic meaning.

Examples ...

Costume – study its quality, fabric, colour, design

Costume		Significance
Coronet, ermine around shoulder, number of dots to show rank		peer/peeress of the realm, entitled to sit in House of Lords; aristocrat
Ecclesiastical robe/robes of office eg Chancellor, cardinal, judge and peers robes = scarlet; cardinal wears square hat, long black robes trimmed with gold		status, honourable qualities, ministerial responsibility
Coronation robes, great cloak lined with ermine and the regalia		emphasis on right to rule rather than on personal qualities
Colour	black	piety, mourning, scholar, cleric
	white	bride/virginity
	pink	femininity
	purple	grand
Armour		military connections; need not indicate fighting had occurred eg decorated armour indicates chivalry
Ring		power, office, loyalty, wealth. Wedding rings were worn on any finger on either hand
Loosely draped dresses, open shirts, hair on shoulders		women with youth, beauty
White skin		breeding
Jewels		
	pearls	wealth, token of love / purity, virginity. Elizabeth I wore them to suggest she was a moon goddess
	diamonds	painted black
Gloves		class/breeding; protecting fair hands from weather

85

'*(Their)...analysis showed that they could use knowledge and skills gained from one subject to develop ideas and skills in another ... I asked students to produce their own self portrait containing a persuasive message of love which required them to use the techniques they had learnt in their art lessons. The art department was given copies of my (history) worksheets, which influenced their production of schemes of work on self portraiture*'.

She also felt that *Who's Been Framed?* had contributed to her personal and professional development through advice and information given by external experts on art and history and using galleries as a resource. She was also helped through contact with other teachers from all sectors and from visiting inspiring places. She thought that the art department had '*woken up to joint concerns in the syllabus*' and the departments have subsequently started to share resources. She learnt that using portraits as evidence is attractive and fun for students and about the value of links between schools and museums and galleries.

Taking the project further

As a result of the project the teacher developed a half term's scheme of work on the Tudors for Year 8 students and changed her approach to teaching the Victorians in Year 9. She planned to incorporate a visit to Montacute House in future. She designed new worksheets and gathered more visual resources, visiting venues such as National Trust properties to do so.

An exhibition of students' work in art and history was staged at the Royal Albert Memorial Museum where 250 people attended the private view. A catalogue documented the project and the exhibition.

Brainstorming for other ideas

Examples of portraits, especially 18th, 19th and early 20th century ones, both paintings and photographs, can be found in most local museums and art galleries and, as the teacher we interviewed discovered, are a fruitful area for research in both art and history.

■ Language development is inherent in almost any project in which students analyse, interpret and discuss objects and images. Working with portraits is no exception. Having looked at historical portraits students might make word portraits of each other, examining individual characteristics as well as aspects of the sitter's experience and pose which characterise the 21st century. Written self portraits might be aspirational. Students might be asked

- How would you like to appear to 21st century viewers?

- What would you like to convey to them?

- What novel, magazine, television programme or film do you think conveys the flavour of our times?

■ An exploration of family photographs, both formal and informal, might reveal the kind of picture that future generations are likely to have of us

- How else might we depict our family?

- What do we want to show about our family?

- What don't we want to show?

- Do formal or informal photographs show family life best?

■ A similar exploration could be made of the ways in which people – usually famous or notorious people – are portrayed in the media, not only through documentary photographs but, for example, through caricature, stamps, memorabilia

- Do they faithfully represent our times?

- Which medium gives a more truthful picture?

- How have the images been manipulated?

■ Having devised a dialogue, story or newspaper article about sitters in two paintings, perhaps from different times, students might write a play incorporating all the different characters their group has looked at. How else can a story be told?

- Puppets?

- Accessories?

- Music?

- Dance?

- Oral history?

■ A study of the changing styles in portraiture might be linked with the social history of the times. Art is not made in isolation. For example:

- What changes did the industrial revolution bring to portraiture?

- How do attitudes to women affect the way they are portrayed?

- Is there a place for the painted portrait in the digital age?

- Did artists such as Renoir, Picasso, Sargent, Gwen John, Stanley Spencer make portraits for the same reason? Would photographs have done the same thing?

WILLIAM MORRIS

What happened?

This project was unusual in that a secondary head teacher initiated it, in order to celebrate the centenary of the death of William Morris, a man who had tried to break down the barriers between fine arts and crafts and promote the notion of arts for all. The head teacher had a keen commitment to the arts '... *the curriculum plan should incorporate arts for personal growth, the development of morality, information handling skills, the observation and under-standing of the environment ... culture, history, occupations ...*[Schools] *should ensure that there is a wide range of the arts and a wide range of modes of putting them across to the students as creators, performers and audience...*'

The culmination of the project was a cross-arts performance.

How did it come about?

The head teacher approached the education and audience development officer for the Orchestra of St John's, Smith Square, who had previously worked with the school. She arranged for the orchestra's composer in residence to work with staff and students. Their musical composition, poetry, and performance skills contributed to the event.

Who was it for?

GCSE and A level music and drama students. The performance was for a general audience.

What was the point?

One of the principal aims was to celebrate the actual centenary day of Morris's death. The **head teacher** was keen to demonstrate '*the complementary interconnection of the arts – the interrelationship between the arts and life – social history in particular*'. He thought that because Morris believed that the arts were not only for a limited range of people he was particularly relevant to students in his multi-cultural inner city school. The **orchestra's** general aims for their educational work are to encourage everyone to use their own creativity and to increase appreciation and enjoyment of the arts, whilst making them more accessible. They wanted to maintain their connection with the school.

90

NORTH WESTMINSTER COMMUNITY SCHOOL
AND THE ORCHESTRA OF ST JOHN'S, SMITH SQUARE
PRESENT

William Morris:
A Centenary Celebration

OCTOBER 3RD, 1996. 6.30 P.M., MARYLEBONE LOWER HOUSE

William Morris

1834   1896

CENTENARY 1996

After the performance, the refreshment bar will be open in the foyer for some time so that members of the audience can see the exhibitions and meet each other.

ENTRANCE IS FREE, BUT THERE WILL BE A COLLECTION ON THE WAY OUT TOWARDS THE EXPENSES.

Programme

1 Welcome and Introduction by Michael Marland

2 *Chanson de Matin* and *Chanson de Nuit*, by Edward Elgar (1857 - 1934) played by the String Quartet of The Orchestra of St John's, Smith Square: Colin Callow and David Smith, violins; Jo St Leon, viola; Nick Roberts, cello

3 Lord Briggs will speak about William Morris

4 *Chaconne in G minor*, by Henry Purcell (1659 - 1695)

5 *Morris the Designer* - a slide sequence of designs by or commissioned by William Morris

6 October, five movements for string quartet inspired by William Morris' poem, composed by Year-Eleven students under the guidance of Cameron Sinclair, who will introduce the work.

   Composers: First Movement: Michael Dritsas; Second: James Evans; Third: Albert Hogg; Fourth: Laura Woolfe; Fifth: Robin Dagsgupta

7 *Morris the Writer, a selection of prose and verse*, performed by the following students: Una Deretic, Hyette Duffy, Alex Elsom, Josie Geddes, Loretta Mogey, Adia Silcox, Natalie Walsh, Jenneth Whitton, Laura Woolfe (Years Ten and Eleven), and Stewart Granger and Gemma Wilcox (Sixth Form)

8 Lord Briggs

9 *Strawberry Thief*, a newly-composed work for string quartet and narrator by Cameron Sinclair. Poem by Anna Burgess (Year Ten); narrator: Gemma Wilcox (Sixth Form)

The foyer exhibition includes wallpaper and fabric designed by Morris, and a selection of early editions of his books kindly loaned by by Henry Sotheran, antiquarian booksellers.

For The Orchestra of St John's, Smith Square: Cameron Sinclair is Composer in Residence; Lucy Heslop is Education Officer.

For North Westminster Community School: The Head of Music, who has led the students' composition work, is Al Hanson, the Head of Drama, who has compiled and directed the spoken presentations, is Karen Palmer; the technician who has hung and operated the lighting is a student who left us last year, Matthew Pountney; the overall Head of Performing Arts is Mark Pattenden.

This event has been sponsored by the City of Westminster Arts, The London Metropole Hotel, and Wordsworth Classics, to all of whom we are very grateful.

This is the programme for the highly ambitious celebration to mark the centenary of William Morris's death put on by students at North Westminster Community School of London.

What did they look at?

To illustrate some aspects of Morris's work, an exhibition of his wallpaper and fabrics and rare early editions of his books, lent by a central London dealer, were displayed in the school foyer. Exhibitions there are a common practice in the school.

How did they prepare?

The drama teacher raised students' awareness of William Morris as a polymath at an introductory weekend course that included talks and the performance of a play written by the head of drama.

What did the students do?

GCSE music students worked with the composer in residence to create a string quartet based on a study of the text of a William Morris poem. A master class was arranged with a cellist from the orchestra and workshops for the school's string players were held.

The head of drama worked with ten GCSE drama students to compile the spoken presentations for the concert. As she did not want the students to perform Morris's works without any insight into them they discussed his political beliefs, in particular his conviction about the right of all people to have access to education and the arts. Unexpectedly, Morris's socialist beliefs were of great interest to the students.

What did people learn?

The musical scores far exceeded expectations and demonstrated the value of working with professional musicians who taped each student's composition for their GCSE coursework.

The composer in residence felt that students had understood the difference in sequencing and composing and that working with professional instrumentalists helped them to '*see the difference between a good idea and a bad one*'.

Drama students studied Morris's love poems and, despite the complex symbolism, enjoyed them. They discovered that the performance of poetry was very different from studying it in an English lesson.

91

Students became aware of Morris as an artist, designer, architect, socialist, writer, poet and teacher. This fascinated them since, in school, these skills are separated into different subject compartments. They thought that Morris's art and taste, which they learned is still popular today, was old fashioned and from another time, although they were excited by his political stance.

On his evaluation sheet the composer wrote that the project was '*proof that an enthusiastic head teacher can work wonders for our position. This project was going to be a success from the start because of the way it was put together*'.

Ideas for taking the project further

The head of drama felt that her students had become very involved in the project and that ideas and concepts gained from it could be discerned in later GCSE course work. Music students' experience led to further original composition.

Brainstorming for other ideas

Visual and written material about and by William Morris is readily available in libraries and museums. As our case study students realised, reproductions of Morris's designs can also be found in many shops. Because he was a polymath, Morris is an ideal focus for a cross curricular project. This school used a composer in residence but it might equally well have been a writer, designer, craftsperson or artist.

- A study of William Morris raises the question of the value of the arts in society today. What is their role? What should it be? Can we call those people who write pop songs poets and composers? Who are the William Morrises of today?

- The discussions that arose about Morris as a socialist might well have taken place in the history department within the context of the industrial revolution, the history of socialism, the trades union movement and the Workers' Education Association. Morris is also relevant to the study of the Victorians at KS2.

- Older students studying the middle ages might look at Morris and pre-Raphaelite interpretations of this era. This could bring out issues about historical interpretation, prejudice and truth.

■ Morris looked to early Renaissance art and design for inspiration. Where do contemporary artists and designers look for their inspiration? How does Victorian design, which Morris reacted against, influence the look of domestic interiors today? Is the influence of the arts and crafts movement and of modernism greater? What do we choose to preserve and value from previous generations?

■ Poetry was used to stimulate musical composition in the case study. It could have led to work in art, craft, design and technology in the form of printmaking and book design with reference to book production at the Kelmscott press and Morris as a poet. Poems could be illustrated with woodcuts, an early form of picture and textile printing, and computer technology could be used as a contrast.

■ Icelandic legends and sagas, another of Morris's interests, might also be a focus for writing interpretive poems and stories, perhaps accompanied by a look at Iceland as a historical and geographical terrain.

WORDS AND WAVES

What happened?

This project demonstrates the value for teachers of having been open to ideas and keeping in touch with what their local museum or art gallery is putting on for schools that might relate to their curriculum.

How did it come about?

The gallery education officer at the Brighton Museum and Art Gallery organised writing workshops to accompany an exhibition of work by the photographer Mark Power called *The Shipping Forecast*. She engaged a writer who was a freelance arts worker and who had been an advisory teacher specialising in story telling and writing. This writer devised the sessions so that they were appropriate for children of all abilities. She also wrote information packs that were sent out to the participating schools.

The teacher we interviewed had introduced the BBC's specialised shipping forecast into his scheme of work for Year 4 geography. He noticed a poster advertising the exhibition of that name and contacted the gallery to find that they were offering writing workshops led by this local writer and educationalist. He was immediately attracted to the idea because it related creative work in English to factual work in geography.

Who was it for?

The workshops were aimed at key stage 2 students.

What was the point?

The workshop was advertised to teachers as a project in which '*Students will be encouraged to respond to these images and to express their feelings through discussion, drawing and writing. Different strategies, such as brainstorming, drafting and conferencing will be explored to develop students' writing towards a finished product. The resulting work will be compiled into a collection*'. This was called *Words and Waves*. The idea was for the students to 'get in to' rather than simply 'look at' the photographs. The writer wanted students to

The exhibition '*The Shipping Forecast*' at Brighton and Hove.

© Mark Power

identify with people and objects and to talk about their perceptions in a focused way. She wanted them all to participate, to use their creativity and to develop their speaking and listening skills as well as their writing skills.

How did they prepare?

Teachers were invited to an introductory twilight teachers' evening. This session also provided suggestions for ways of developing students' draft materials into different forms of writing. Participating schools were sent material, including photocopies of the photographs, to support the work undertaken in the gallery.

The students in this case study had already studied rivers and visited the beach, the local River Adur, and had met a representative from Southern Water. Work was then extended out from the locality to seas and oceans.

Because he was particularly interested in sailing, the teacher introduced the theme of weather at sea, bringing into school a weather at sea manual and a recording of the BBC's shipping forecast. The students were given a photocopied map of the sea areas and learnt their names and locations. They were also taught about wind direction and speed, and were expected to be able to plot these on their maps.

Richard French from Mowden School, Sussex wrote this poem for the publication that Brighton Museum and Art Gallery's education staff prepared to mark their work during the exhibition *The Shipping Forecast*, photographs by Mark Power.

Tyne
Tuesday 27 July 1993
South 3 veering southwesterly 4 or 5.
Occasional rain. Moderate occasionally poor

There I was
On the beach
Waiting for some wet sand and water
When a wave came.

A huge ample wave hit me
Smashed me to the ground.
I lay there.
Still.
I don't move.
I feel so, so sad and grim as
I lie there motionless in fright.

I sit there,
I'm smelly and I reek of seaweed.
I can't move a muscle.
I sit there
Like a lump of jelly.

I am scared.
I want my Mum and Dad.
I want to talk or shout.
But I can't
I just can't move at all.

Richard French
Mowden School

Reference notes for students provided by the writer leading the *Words and Waves* workshops.

Words and Waves

Notes on the writing process

1. Gather ideas – visualise an object or place or event or look at a photograph.

2. Brainstorm – write down any thoughts you may have about the subject

3. Burstwrite – in a strict time limit write and write and write – everything that comes into your head. Don't stop to think – just write. It can help to give each thought a separate line. Burstwriting is a kick-start into writing

4. Spiderchart – write down the subject in the centre of the page and link your thoughts to the title with lines. (This can happen as a result of burst writing).

Next:
<u>Think</u> of your audience – who is the writing for? Is it a person from the past, the future, the present, someone younger, someone older?
Think of a a possible form: Is it going to be a story, a poem, a letter, a diary extract a newspaper report, a video storyboard, a script for a radio programme?

Then:
- Highlight – underline the words you want to use
- Draft – write in double spacing so that you can edit easily
               and/or
    - photocopy the draft so that the draft can be cut and stuck
    - eliminate superfluous words e.g. 'and' & 'then' etc
- Edit – check the meaning – spelling and punctuation and capital letters at this stage.

<u>Read</u> – read your work aloud to a friend and listen to check the punctuation and meaning. Ask your friend to comment on your work and note the comments if you find them helpful. Sometimes it is useful just to read your writing out loud to someone else, and to listen to their writing too. Think of two good things to say about the writing, and a question about the meaning which might be helpful.

<u>Publish</u> – present your work   -   decorate it for a wall display
                                    -   as a booklet on its own
                                    -   as part of a collection of writing

Carole Mason w/w 1997

97

What did they look at?

The focus for the workshop was an exhibition of large scale photographs by Mark Power. Although objectively named and dated according to the shipping forecast area where they were taken, they differed greatly in their subject matter and mood. Some showed people in surprising, and even disturbing, situations and they were taken from a variety of different angles and perspectives.

What did the students do?

At the gallery, as an icebreaker they discussed the function of the shipping forecast and listened to a tape of it, this time thinking about the feelings invoked by the rhythms of sound, voice and music. These first impressions were reinforced by the soundtracks of broadcasts, waves and storms which accompanied the exhibition.

Students worked in the public galleries during opening hours, and this made their activities quite a public event. They looked round the exhibition and chose three photographs before explaining their choices to a partner. At this point the writer introduced the idea of brain-storming and modelled this with the whole group before small groups used the technique to look at two photographs each. A scribe recorded the words and phrases they came up with which students then used in individual pieces of 'burst writing' lasting from five to ten minutes. These could be written from the point of view of a person or an object in the chosen photograph. After everyone shared their work with their group, their teacher and with the writer, volunteers read out their pieces to the whole class as examples of possible approaches to the organisation of a poem.

Students who found the exercise difficult were given a framework on paper within which to draw a story board, picking out the features of an image and then inventing what might have taken place before the picture was taken and what might happen next. They then added words to their drawings.

The session concluded with a small piece of 'think writing' about their experience in the gallery.

What did people learn?

The writer thought that the **students** had very much enjoyed sharing ideas and talking about Mark Power's photographs with their peers and with her as a writer. It was felt that the workshop had consolidated and built upon existing knowledge which manifested itself in the recall of images and place names. This group of students had gained extra confidence from their background knowledge of the shipping forecast and was able to connect up disparate elements more easily than students who came fresh to it. The **teacher** liked the workshop's structured approach and he and his colleague, who took the writing forward, gained much from seeing an experienced writer at work with their students.

Taking the project further

As the writer's teaching methods had drawn out such a positive response from both the students and the teachers, producing finished pieces for Words and Waves back in school posed no problems. Students used their computer skills to give a professional finish to their work.

The teacher thought that the group had been so successful in the gallery that they were chosen as guinea pigs for a geography and science residential field trip in which discussion and socialisation were to help the process of recording and classification.

99

Brainstorming for other ideas

In our case study the cross curricular success of the *Words and Waves* writing workshop was to some extent due to the support of preparatory work done in geography lessons.

■   One of the points we want to make is that photographs can be stimulating for observation and interpretation in geography as well as design and technology and in English.

•   Landscape photographers, such as Fay Godwin or Hamish Fulton, can be used for interpreting weather conditions, soil, vegetation and climate.

•   Students could look at the work of local artists or at photography archives in museums and compare the 'constructed' landscape with the actual environment.

- They could try to make maps from paintings or photographs, using appropriate symbols. This might lead to discussion about coded languages – drawings, paintings cartoons or advertisements contain their own coded languages like maps – and to the creation of a new language of symbols, perhaps related to giving directions to a stranger from outer space.

- In reverse, students might construct a landscape painting or model from information given on an ordnance survey map.

- The names of farms, villages, rivers and so on printed on the map, might be used as a stimulus for story writing, artwork or historical research.

■ The exhibition, *The Shipping Forecast*, included background sound. Students could devise sound effects or compose music to accompany an exhibition of their own art, photographs or written work which might be based on very precise descriptions of weather conditions at particular dates and times. They could record, photographically, the same site over a period of time, showing the effect that different weather and light conditions have on landscape, trees and buildings. Or their exhibition might consist of carefully researched and constructed maps of the school environment, using measurement and scale and appropriate recordings.

■ Students' contributions to *Words and Waves* were put together by gallery staff to form a booklet. Using computer technology, individual collections of creative writing, drawings and photographs about the local environment could, with the help of a Bookbinder in School, be made into books.

5

Deciding where to go

The purpose of this chapter is to help people who may be planning a school visit for the first time to choose a location that will support the work being done in school. It also suggests some things that teachers can look out for if they want to break the mould of their traditional school trip.

Most schools take students out on visits to museums and galleries at some point during the school year. Once a school has made a successful visit, they often repeat that visit year after year. However, our case studies have shown that popular topics such as water, light, portraits, the Victorians or the Second World War can benefit from new approaches and themes.

Finding out about what is on offer

The first stage in deciding where to go is finding out what is on offer locally and further afield. Local directories will give the addresses and phone numbers of museums and galleries. Colleagues and advisory staff may be able to offer advice. As the case studies included in this book show, there are many excellent local or regional museums and galleries that can be used to support a wide range of curriculum themes. It is certainly not always necessary to organise a coach to the nearest metropolis in order to find Egyptian collections, contemporary art or live interpretation.

To find out about local temporary and permanent exhibitions and the possibilities they can offer, teachers need to get themselves personally on mailing lists and make themselves and their interests known. It is really hard for organisers to target their mailshots effectively and they will welcome a direct approach.

The teacher we interviewed for *Words and Waves* had, by keeping his ear to the ground, heard about a one-off creative writing workshop that related to what his students were doing in geography. However, in doing so, he became more aware of what his local museum had to offer and of the general potential of relating creative work in English to factual work in geography. He also found out for himself the benefits of working in a gallery with a different style of teaching.

A willingness to respond quickly can lead to exciting gallery experiences for teachers and students. The teacher who attended the *Art and Dance* workshop run in association with a temporary exhibition of contemporary painting was attracted to it '*because it was spontaneous, having been prepared and advertised very quickly with energy and excitement*'.

Outlines for the projects that formed the case studies sometimes arose from individual, idiosyncratic research and planning either on the part of the museum educator or of the teacher, as in *Art and Dance* or *Splash! The Egyptians* is another good example. Here the art education officer at the museum designed a half day session in the Egyptian gallery both to respond to the school's request to '*do something with the Egyptians*' and to fulfil a desire on her own part to '*get underneath the skin of the Egyptian display*'.

Of course, projects also arise from more structured research, consultation and piloting, as in the case of *Back to the Future* and *Strike a Light*. They might be large scale like *Who's Been Framed?* or small scale like *Words and Waves*. They might even be a unique unit within a large scale education programme as in *Braque*. Indeed initiatives need not come from the museum, gallery or arts organisation but can come from the school. This happened in the *William Morris* case study. Some projects such as *Strike a Light* and *Swansea at War* can be repeated with stimulating additions and alterations year after year. Whatever the background, cross curricular projects using museum objects and images arise from a knowledge of what and who can contribute. This knowledge leads to an informed choice of topic and an awareness of potential.

Gallery and museum staff

Once the range of possibilities has been identified the next task is to narrow the choice and establish which one is best suited to the needs of students and colleagues. Many teachers look for places which have professional staff who can offer taught sessions or who can help them to plan their visit. Chapter 2 looked at the support that can be offered. It is always worth asking whether there is someone who can work with students. Museums and galleries that do not have their own education staff may well use freelancers.

Artists

For example, many museums and galleries work with practising artists. Chapter 2 also looked at the benefits to students of working with them, and the case studies show some of the projects that can result. Artists in Schools might be associated with a gallery, as in *Casting Shadows*, or with another arts organisation such as an orchestra, as in *William Morris*. Museums and galleries do organise Artists in Schools and sometimes have an in-house artist in residence doing work related to their collections or exhibitions programme. Artists might work directly with students, as in the *Art and Dance* and *Words and Waves* projects, or give performances about a topic theme, as in *Swansea at War*. Funding initiatives, such as the Year of the Artist in year 2000, offer many opportunities for placements.

103

Information about arts organisations' education services, details of galleries and museums that run residencies and names of artists who work either in schools or in museums and galleries comes from a variety of sources. Regional Arts Boards, LEAs, or local authority Arts, Cultural, Leisure or Library Services can be contacted.

Supporting materials

This initial research phase can also be used to find out about supporting materials. This might be written material produced by LEA advisors, as was the case with *Who's Been Framed?* but it could also take the form of teachers' packs, gallery guides, catalogues, videos or even CD Roms produced in galleries or museums. In the case of *Strike a Light*, as well as teachers' notes, there was a supplementary resource pack, which gave in depth information about the history of light and the science of light and colours.

An evaluation of teachers' packs in ten London museums and galleries showed that many teachers simply do not know about the range of packs available in their area (Sue Clive and Petra Geggie, 1998).

A round of phone calls to local and national museums can reveal dozens of relevant publications, and these are often available free of charge. Enquiries at gallery and museum shops (where postcards, posters, catalogues, resource packs and books are stocked) will show what other resources can be found to support a proposed topic. It is certainly worth keeping an eye out for gallery leaflets and guides produced for the general visitor.

Support materials might be produced for a specific aspect of a collection or an exhibition, as in the case of *Braque* and *Back to the Future*, but they may well be transferable to other projects. This happened in *The Egyptians* where a primary level teachers' pack, together with postcards and posters, gave factual background and visual reminders to inform secondary school art students' work. Packs often include activity or work sheets. These can be used directly or adapted for particular students and selected themes. Many teachers appreciate that a teacher's pack has a long shelf life and can be used for more than one project.

Using real objects, handling and loan collections

Working with real objects helps to make a museum or gallery visit different from classroom activities. As well as the wonderful range of items on permanent or temporary display, the research phase will also show whether there are interactive exhibits, handling or loan collections and what they contain. Loan collections should never replace the museum visit. They can, however, be used to stimulate discussion amongst colleagues and help to decide the questions to be discussed and the themes to be explored (see below) during a project. They can also be used to introduce a project in school and contribute to follow up work.

Our (adult) focus groups found handling objects very exciting

> *I find it brilliantly exciting to touch real objects. Handling gives another dimension. They are very exciting to touch not just because they are shoes but because they are aesthetic things. They are so old, that is important.*

Making an exploratory visit

Much of this research can be done over the telephone or by letter and fax or searching on the web. However, before finally deciding on the topic, and certainly before settling on the themes to be explored at school and at the museum or gallery, it really helps to make a visit and, if possible, meet the staff. Obviously, such visits are best made with other colleagues. It is a chance to see what is on offer and to start discussing how the collections can be used with students. This visit is discussed more fully in the next chapter.

Good projects frequently emerge from proactive approaches made by teachers. For *Strike a Light* a small group of primary teachers approached the museum education service with a request for more activities and resources for KS1 students. They were looking for exciting ways in which to involve them in working with museum objects and introduce them to simple concepts about light and energy.

6

Planning a cross curricular project

All the case studies used in this book demonstrate the rewards that come from careful planning. This chapter looks in detail at the planning process and gives clear ideas for ways to turn a run-of-the-mill outing into a stimulating and memorable learning experience.

The key issues to discuss are:

- deciding why the visit is being made,

- what the learning outcomes are going to be,

- what themes will be explored,

- how these relate to areas of the curriculum

- what objects the students should be using

Our research has shown that these aspects are best addressed on site and by as many people as possible. Only after this process is complete is it time to think of a date for the visit and book the coach.

The advantages of brainstorming

The most creative projects and the best ideas for cross curricular work develop out of brainstorming sessions amongst people from different specialisms and with different interests and

108

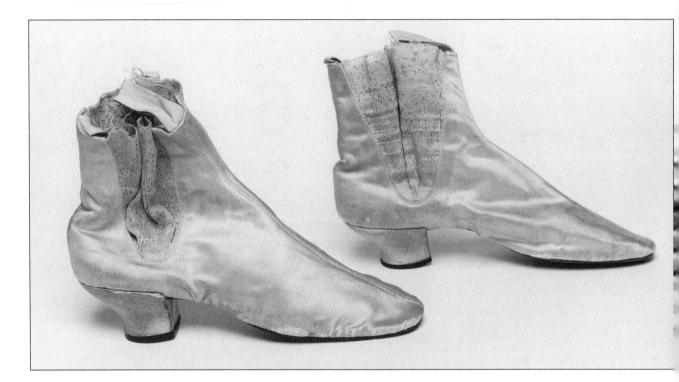

skills. The focus groups showed that, if educators get together to look at objects and talk about them, exciting new teaching ideas will emerge or familiar topics will be given new life and emphasis. It really is worth while getting colleagues together in the museum or gallery as a form of research and development for cross curricular work. It may best be based around a professional development day or INSET session but the results will certainly justify the effort. A brainstorming session at the very beginning of the planning process encourages the kind of lateral thinking needed to break out from a closed subject specialism into

Above: A pair of Victorian silk shoes and opposite a medieval leather one from the handling collection at the Museum of London. To understand the value of brainstorming, these shoes provoked discussions covering women's experiences, technology, urban history, dance and drama, conservation and archaeology as well as the role of imagination.
(The Museum of London)

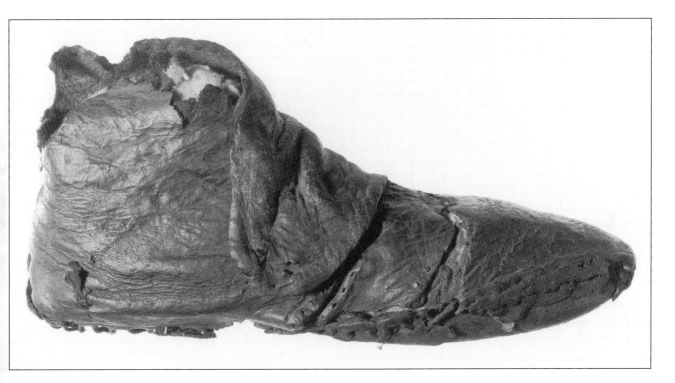

the cross curricular approach. It is fun and infinitely more rewarding than trying to do it single handedly.

As an example of the powers of brainstorming, one of our focus groups looked at two very different shoes; a medieval leather shoe and a Victorian silk one

Neither of us had any professional knowledge to get us started ... We imagined that they might have something to do with women's experience at different times ...This one is a wonderful example of how, without knowing anything about technology, you can work out how it is made ... It is full of clues. You can see how the leather has been folded round and held together. We talked a bit about urban history and the place where the shoe might have been worn ... places where there is mud, where you would need this sort of stiff shoe for protection. The other one is not wearable in mud. It is to be worn indoors or where there is a pavement.

We talked about how you could get students to look at the details of the objects, for example the worn bit on the side of this shoe. Get them using their imaginations about how it got there. 'Was it a bunion?' for example. These details are nice because they show the relationship between the imagined body and our own body. You would behave differently wearing these shoes. You could take that into dance or drama. We talked quite a bit about the role of imagination and what kinds of things stimulate the imagination. Is it an adult shoe that cramped the toes together, or is it a child's? We all assumed that it was a woman's shoe but there are plenty of pictures of men wearing shoes like this. We even discussed whether the leather shoe is a shoe at all or whether it is a last.

You could look at conservation and preservation and how and why some things survive. One of them has been preserved in water or something like that; for some reason it has been in a situation where it has been preserved. What materials decay first? The threads have gone on this one. It also makes you think about what materials were available at the time. Where did they come from? There are all sorts of historical associations to do with trade that you could explore. (Focus Group, Museum of London)

110 Brainstorming helps participants to tune into the different teaching and learning experiences which are available and encourages them to start thinking about the kinds of on site activities their students might undertake. Moreover, it promotes an enthusiasm that cannot come from simply discussing it in the staff room. This enthusiasm contributes to the success of a visit and enriches all the work that the students are doing right across the curriculum.

Our examples show the range of people who can enliven the discussion process. The brainstorming for *Back to the Future* involved teachers, museum staff and advisory teachers. One of the teachers involved said '*I would never have thought of using a museum for science unless it was a science collection. This project helped me see the science behind the history*'.

Developing the learning objectives

The learning objectives for a visit to a museum or gallery might be very different from those in school. One of the fundamental reasons for going on a visit has to be that there are things that students can only do or achieve through working in the galleries. This fact will determine the learning objectives.

What makes visiting a museum or gallery different is the excitement of working with objects. One of the key objectives should be that students work with, study and learn from the collections even though research in the archives or the library may be an integral part of the visit. If they leave the museum or gallery with the information, skills and ideas that could just as easily have been obtained from a study of photographs or textbooks in the classroom then the visit cannot be considered a real success.

One of the teachers who attended *In Touch with the Past* commented on how much she valued the different learning outcomes afforded her students. She said that she had brought students to the museum because she knew it would enable them to touch on a wide range of subject areas.

Focusing on objects and images means that teachers need to be very clear just what their students can learn from the collections. After that, they will be in a position to decide when they will need access to support material or to other primary sources. The nature of the objects also impacts both on the preparation needed before the visit and the follow up.

On site work should:

111

    Be object centered
    Set clear learning outcomes which students are aware of
    Ask open ended questions that stimulate students to ask their own questions
    Review the learning that has taken place

Learning outcomes should:

    Be securely embedded in classroom work and not a one-off
    Start from students' experience and knowledge and build on this
    Require and value a range of responses
    Be achievable but also stretch the students
    Be truly cross curricular
    Be flexible

Encourage careful looking
Involve students in both acquiring and using skills, concepts and knowledge
Involve students in finding things out for themselves
Involve students in active learning
Offer a variety of experiences

The social benefits of the visit to should not be neglected. The experience of the visit includes working in groups in a public space, interacting with the museum staff and visiting the shop. The journey to the museum can be used to develop planning and map-reading skills. Students can consult timetables, contact the museum information desk and even book the visit if these are skills that the teacher wants to develop.

The case study that looks at a group of French students who visited the Braque exhibition at the Royal Academy demonstrates how many different learning objectives can be encompassed by one visit. The gallery education officer wanted to develop speaking and listening skills. She wanted the students to use language creatively to describe aspects of the paintings such as content, composition and mood. She wanted the students to consider Braque's techniques and working processes and to draw attention to the way in which his paintings were made and how they are open to different interpretations. She planned to put this in a general historical and art historical background. However, the school had an extra objective. The teacher said that '*at school we don't open minds – it is important to see other things, part of our culture*'.

Are additional resources such as photographs or documents essential to achieve the learning outcomes? If so at what stage are they to be made available? Some museums and galleries have teaching rooms for additional research on site, others may well provide access to their library, their handling collections, catalogues or stores. When planning the visit teachers need to be aware of what facilities are available even if they decide not to use them.

Opposite: There needs to be something intriguing. You have to be able to say 'here are some stories'. These building blocks showing children from all over the world with a white child on top provoked plenty of discussion at the Museum of London. (Museum of London)

112

Planning follow up work

It is also necessary to think about follow up work at the planning stage because it has important implications for the preparations beforehand as well as for the actual visit. If it is ignored teachers may well find they would like to make the whole visit again.

However, it is impossible to plan everything that will be done after the trip because a good visit will have so enthused and stimulated students that they will have their own ideas about following up and extending the project. Nonetheless, the work done on site should provide students with the information they need to take the project further. Chapter 4 looks at some additional ways in which the case study visits might have been followed up in school. We wanted to show how the benefits of the visit could be spread to other areas of the curriculum. We brainstormed for this.

The museum or gallery may well be able to help with ideas for follow up work if it is discussed with them in advance. Some institutions will lend objects to schools, as in *William Morris*. Others might provide display space so that students can put on an exhibition of their

work, as in *Casting Shadows.* For *Words and Waves* the gallery produced a booklet of students' poems. Such events can turn a day's outing into a life long memory.

Choosing objects and displays

I go through a list of factors in my head when thinking about which objects to use. There are certain checkpoints. There has to be some intrinsic mystery which helps people get into it – something intriguing – some kind of symbolism to make use of. You have to be able to say 'here are some stories'. (Focus group, Museum of London)

The brainstorming session will have thrown up a whole range of possible themes to explore on the actual visit. Once a final choice has been made the group can start to think about which display cases or parts of the exhibition are going to be used and which objects are going to be the focus. Remember, though, that it is usually impractical for a whole class of students to crowd around the same case or image and it may be best to plan for students to work in groups.

a. Familiar objects or new ones?

There is a choice whether or not to start students off with the kind of objects they recognise, and to work from these to things that are new and different or whether to show them objects they won't have seen before and might not recognise. Two of our focus groups had a tea cup as one of their objects but each was very different and provoked contrasting reactions.

The focus group at the Museum of London had an Edwardian cup

Our immediate response was that this [the cup] was really boring, whereas this [a Roman tile with animal footprints on it] was quite exciting. It is useful to have an initial familiarity with objects but in this case I am almost too familiar with it. I know what it is. If I were a child and had been given the cup rather than the tile I would have felt really let down. The tile is much more exciting; it is a bit of a mystery.

However the cup which the group at Leighton House was given proved much more rewarding, probably because the imagery on it provided that element of mystery identified as so important by the first group. The imagery had a resonance for the people looking at it which provoked a lot of discussion.

114

We looked at the cup first ...The first thing that struck us was that it has an image on it which refers to slavery and which the anti-slavery movement used as a logo. It has a different meaning to us now. It doesn't acknowledge the part black people played in resisting slavery. Then I wondered if the cup was produced by anti-slavery campaigners, at the time it must have been quite an aggressive thing to have ... it could have been quite a controversial thing to have on the tea table saying 'actually I'm not in favour of slavery'. Except that people could just have read it as a picture of interesting natives, a nice tame black person. Astonishing to see something all about the history of slavery being contained in one object – exoticism, the tea trade, the development of the Empire, western wealth, abolition of slavery, the concept of the logo, etc.

A chocolate cup printed with images of slavery that the focus group held at Leighton House discussed.

Cup, private collection. Photograph, © John W. Rogers.

Whatever the decision about using familiar or unfamiliar objects it is important to recognise that at some point students will need and want to know what something is and what it was used for. Working out what a mystery object is has a point, but until that question is answered, it is impossible to move on to finding out more about the people who made it, or used it, or owned it.

b. Objects are displayed in a context

Museums and galleries rarely display objects in isolation. A display or exhibition in a museum or gallery makes different statements, both explicit and implicit, through the choice of objects, their place in the case or room and in relation to each other and the interpretation they have been given. In an article he wrote in 1994, Ray Batchelor describes looking at his own 1910 electric kettle and the potential it had for stimulating discussion about its invention, manufacture, materials, marketing, design and use. He wonders, however, whether a museum visitor who saw the kettle in a 1910 drawing room display would look as carefully at it and discover as much about it.

Mrs. Pankhurst gave this bronze medal to Mary Richardson, the suffragette who slashed Velasquez's painting known as the 'Rokeby Venus' in the National Gallery. It is inscribed 'SACRIFICE FOR WOMEN'S RIGHTS 1914' and has a scene in relief of force feeding. Our focus group emphasised how a single object can often stimulate a range of responses – the basis of an exciting cross curricular project.

The Museum of London

Standing in front of this case filled with suffragette ephemera some of our focus group believed that a single object could stimulate better questions and discussion.

The Museum of London

117

Our focus groups made much the same point. One group, working with a case of ephemera and objects on the theme of the suffragettes, noted that

> *This case seems to be trying to convey a sense of the injustice that people labour under at certain points ... but it has become a kind of antique shop and you get no sense of involvement with the ideal. This is just a load of junk. The potential of the objects to excite and take people in different directions is cut out. If you had just that chain belt and tin cup and took away all the rest, you'd get much more from them.*

c. The value of comparison

Our focus group participants frequently talked about the value of opportunities to compare and contrast objects in museums and galleries and about bringing everyday objects into museums so that students can compare them with what is on display. Comparison can encourage closer observation of objects and increase understanding of function, use and design. It can also stimulate conjecture about how else the object might have looked and about continuity and change. In *The Egyptians*, the art education officer invited students to compare Egyptian artefacts with work by a contemporary artist. She wanted to encourage responses that students would use to inform their own art work.

d. Objects tell stories

Some objects invite discussion through the stories attached to them or through their power to stimulate the imagination. This can be distracting of course. One group, working with a large toy building brick which was covered with images of children from all over the world with a white boy on the top, found that they '*got stuck on those horrible little pictures rather than thinking about bricks or boxes*' (Focus group, Museum of London)

A unique aspect of working with objects is that they either have histories that can be revealed or they can inspire people to speculate about them. Both can be used to support the teaching of literacy. This is how the group at Leighton House speculated about the photograph album

> *The album is monumental and very intriguing because unless you see the side or the end you don't necessarily see it as a book. It is like a tomb. It could be a box so the idea of Pandora's box came up ... I was interested about what you might anticipate was inside ... the*

contrast between expectation and reality ... We thought that as an object it is so fascinating that it would lend itself to some story telling about the history of the object or anything in it. It has connotations of myth and legend.

Many of the focus group members talked about how the objects they were working with stimulated them to talk about the people who might have made them or used them or owned them. The group looking at the photograph album also pointed out

What is interesting in the family groups is the hierarchy, where people are sitting and how they are placed ...The thing about these photographs is that people had to keep very still so they look very stern. If you don't know about it, it gives you a certain view of the Victorians ... It would be interesting to get children thinking about who the woman is and what she is thinking. What kind of life does she lead? Her work is going to be very different from their mother's work. Look at her hands.

Deciding when to visit the museum or gallery

The project's aims should dictate at which stage the visit will be most useful and effective. The conventional approach is to visit at the beginning of a topic to stimulate excitement and interest in a way that will have impact and inform it as a whole. But it is worth reviewing this assumption as the details of the visit are fleshed out.

119

The students' visit to the art gallery for the *Art and Dance* case study was intended to give teachers something they could take on and develop. As the dancer who led the project pointed out, many people teaching dance in schools are primarily PE teachers rather than dance specialists and they look at dance forms such as ballet, tap and modern dance from the technical rather than the creative and educational point of view.

However, a visit in the middle of a topic can stimulate fresh interest and provide a new focus for different approaches. The gallery visit for *Words and Waves* took place when the students had been thoroughly grounded in a study of oceans, seas, rivers, canals and the BBC's shipping forecasts. This grounding provided a sound basis for looking at the photography exhibition, coincidentally called *The Shipping Forecast*, and interpreting it through creative writing.

For *Splash!,* the children had several sessions at the gallery and at their nursery school. They discussed watery paintings at both venues and the whole project was intended to emphasise the desirable outcomes of speaking and listening and of investigating and making. The focus of the project was the process of making and interpreting an exhibition.

A different kind of visit might take place to round off a project – to celebrate it, develop students' confidence and pride in achievement and help facilitate future learning. This was the case in *Casting Shadows*. In *You've Been Framed* the teachers' achievements were also celebrated.

7

Working on site

This chapter looks at some of the practical areas for teachers to think about when preparing and running a visit. It focuses on preparing students and on strategies for getting them to look closely at objects and work confidently with them.

Preparing students and adult helpers

Some students may not have been to a museum or gallery before; others may see them in a very negative light. A survey undertaken among non-visitors (*Dingy Places and Different Kinds of Bits*, 1991) revealed that many 16 to18 year olds had very negative views of art galleries and museums which stemmed from earlier visits they had made as students.

The ability to look at and learn from objects is not innate. It is a skill that has to be acquired. Preparing students to visit an art gallery or a museum therefore means introducing the skills they will need in the galleries. They will also need to be given background concepts and information to carry out the tasks they are to be set.

A Teachers' Guide to Learning from Objects (Gail Durbin, Susan Morris, Sue Wilkinson, 1990) is a useful publication from English Heritage that contains a section on classroom activities based around ordinary household objects which can be used to teach the skills of close observation, questioning and analysis. In much the same way children have to be taught to look at and analyse paintings to have the confidence to talk about what they see and what it might mean.

Many school visits rely on the help and support of parents and carers to supervise children. These adult helpers also need to be prepared for the visit. Like the students, they need to know what to expect from the day and they also need to know how they can contribute to its success.

It is helpful to prepare a sheet for them which sets out the learning outcomes for the day and gives them a timetable. They also find it useful to have some information about the museum or gallery being visited and how the visit is going to relate to work in school. Above all, they need to know what the students are going to be doing, why they are doing it and how they can help them. For example, if you don't want adult helpers to tell students the answers to the questions you have set, then you need to tell them this and perhaps offer some guidance about what to do when children ask for help. An adult helper can be invaluable in directing students' attention, praising and encouraging them and asking questions that will stimulate close observation and discovery. However, they can only do this if they have been adequately briefed and prepared. An adult helper can also act as a reader and scribe for the group so that the students can concentrate on looking and talking whilst still having a record of the visit. This can form part of the report-back session, which can be planned to take place at the end of the visit, or later in school.

On arrival

Students need to be briefed on arrival about plans for the session, either by their teacher or a member of the museum staff if available. Students should be told again why they are there – what they are going to do, how it relates to work back at school and what will be expected of them during the course of the day. They should also be briefed about the programme for the day including lunch and toilet breaks and visits to the museum shop. Most museum and gallery rules are based on common sense (not running in the galleries, not touching the objects) so students could be asked to generate them for themselves. They might also need to be reminded that these are places where they are welcome to talk quietly about objects rather than places for silence.

Icebreakers

Museums and galleries are unfamiliar places for many people. Chapter 6 looks at ways of preparing students for the experience but it is also useful to spend the first few minutes of a visit letting students get their bearings. An icebreaker helps them to focus on what they will be doing during their visit. It is designed to get students into the right frame of mind for looking at and working with objects. As such, it does not need to concentrate on the actual objects students will be working with. It can use other objects or it can be based on their own experiences.

It should be an easy task to which everyone can contribute. It gives students 'permission to speak' in an unfamiliar and often quiet and intimidating environment. It helps to motivate them in an informal way. It is a way of making introductions to the museum or gallery educators and adult helpers. In a relaxed way, the 'icebreaker' gives students a sense of what they are going to be thinking about and looking for later. Like most museum and gallery activities, it helps to develop good speaking and listening skills.

As an introduction to an exhibition of photographs by Fay Godwin, *Our Forbidden Land*, students considered '*the idea of irregular shapes as opposed to regular ones in the landscape and identified some of them, making a list of regular shapes*'. The icebreaker session introduced a vocabulary they might use in discussion in front of the photographs later. Then they talked about '*the reasons why Fay Godwin might have selected particular images, chosen particular shapes and ... the effect that combinations of shapes had on the overall composition and atmosphere*'.

The students' teacher appreciated the value of the icebreaker.

> *The discussion, or 'buzz' session preceding the viewing of Fay Godwin's photographic exhibition was particularly worthwhile. David initiated the whole range of language pertaining to the environment, its shape, and the feelings it might evoke as well as setting the scene for a walk round the exhibition.* (Norman Binch and Sue Clive, 1994)

An alternative is to devise specific ice breaking activities that link students' own experience to the collections they have come to study. The journey to the gallery provided material for

123

setting the scene for an exhibition of contemporary Australian Aboriginal art at Corner-house, Manchester. Since traditional Aboriginal paintings refer to actual and mythological journeys, students were asked in turn to remember something they had seen or experienced on their trip to the gallery. The workshop session which followed also took the form of a journey round the gallery following clues and stopping off for discussion about the artworks. For practical work, the students made a map of this journey through three galleries. They had to find ways of representing the whole experience visually.

Looking carefully

Once the students have relaxed and begun to feel comfortable, it is important to spend a little time getting them used to looking closely at objects and how to find out more about them. This can be done through the types of questions students are asked, or it can be done as a separate exercise before students start work on the main activities of the day.

A strategy to encourage younger students to use their eyes is to play observation games. For example, they can be asked to look for something that they think no one else will have noticed so that they can point it out to the rest of the group. Such games establish the principle of careful looking. The children's leaflet *Beginners' Guide to Braque* used this strategy. Students were asked to look at the paintings and to find easel shapes within them.

KS1 students who were visiting a gallery to study German Expressionist prints had a first look at the exhibition in small groups

> *Writing down key words about what they saw – not opinions, but things they noticed immediately such as 'black and white' or 'squiggly lines'. From this, they noticed the wood grain, wood splits and the mark-making peculiar to woodcuts, which led to an understanding of how the pictures were made.* (Norman Binch and Sue Clive 1994)

Strategies for looking can be devised that make it seem as if the students are in control of the choice of objects to look at in detail but which actually guide them towards the objects – or groups of objects – already identified as a focus for study at the planning stage.

During a general, introductory look at an exhibition or display, it is useful if students are given a simple task to encourage them to explore and notice things. In *The Egyptians*, students were asked to go round the room and find something that they found odd, confusing or interesting. They had to be able to explain the reasons for their choice before making two or three large scale charcoal or pastel drawings of it.

As we have seen in Chapter 3, comparing and contrasting objects is a good strategy for encouraging close observation and the discussions that are an aid to learning. For example, one of our focus groups compared a19th century photograph of Lord Leighton's studio with the same room as it is presented now that Leighton House is a museum open to the public. This activity led to a 'now and then' speculative exploration.

> *We thought that the photographs were a representation of what it was like but they don't appear to be at all. It appears to be a kind of romanticised chaos really. And why were these pictures taken? Was Leighton still alive when they were taken? Initially they looked as if they were more full of life than the present day room because the room is now emptied out. They somehow had the sense of being more authentic. But this we quickly dismantled. When we looked closely they both seemed equally false. The fact that there are no people makes them like stage sets – a kind of display. Are you saying that he kind of posed his studio? Yes. That's what it feels like. It is what artists did at the time. It was like their shop window where they sold the goods – the business. The whole of the house is like a temple to that idea. We started talking about the artist's studio and what is an artist? Do they have studios like this today? It's an image. He's selling the whole deal. Damien Hirst is doing it today. He has an office – the media – the same stuff but a different way of doing it.* (Focus group, Leighton House)

125

Asking Questions

Once the scene has been set whether through icebreakers, looking strategies or both, it is time to start looking more closely at the chosen objects. Judicious questions, whether written or spoken, encourage careful looking, thinking and discussing around the topic or theme.

On visits to *Strike a Light* group leaders were provided with a set of questions that focused attention on how the different lights were designed and how they worked

The focus group at Leighton House contrasted Lord Leighton's
studio as it is today (above) with the photograph of it taken in the
painter's life time (right) and raised an enormous range of questions
(Leighton House, London)

What is it made from? How does it feel? Does it smell? What could it be used for? Is it a light? Where does the light come from? What makes the light? Is it fire or something else? If it is a light, is it an oil lamp, a rush light, a candle, a gas or paraffin light or an electric light? If it is not fire, then what form of energy makes the light?

Many of these questions are closed questions. Closed questions are ones which are designed to elicit either a 'yes/no' or an 'I don't know' response. They imply that there is a correct answer to the question. Closed questions can encourage observation and discovery about, for example, materials, methods and function but they can also shut down discussion and discourage those who don't think they know the proper answer from participating.

Asking questions. Some of our focus group members had asked us whether paintings, as distinct from objects, could be used as source material for cross curricular work. Paintings are not only about art and art history and you can ask the same kinds of questions about them as many of our case studies show.

	Objects	Images
What is it?	Two shoes	A picture of the General Post Office
What does it look like?	Height? Length? Colour? Shape? Texture?	Height? Breadth? Length? Colours? Content? Texture?
What is it made of?	Leather? Wood? Silk? Thread? Buttons? Wool? Linen? Metal? Lace?	Paint? Watercolours? Pastels? Found Objects? Wood? Metal? Canvas? Crayons? Paper? Charcoal? Crayons?
How was it made?	By hand? Using a machine? Quickly? Slowly? From a design?	Oil paint? Water colour/Brush? Palette knife? From drawings? From life? From imagination?
Why was it made?	To wear? To sell? To show off? To look nice? For display? For ritual?	To sell? To look at? To commemorate an event? For publicity? To tell a story?
Who made it?	A crafts person? The wearer? A fashion house? A boot maker? An assembly line?	An artist? A commercial artist? An amateur? An academician? Someone famous?
Who was it made for?	A worker? Someone rich? A man? A woman? A child? A museum? A customer? A company?	A rich person? The post office? An official? A middle class person? A patron? A man? A woman? A museum?

What clues can be used to date it?	Fashion? Materials? Method of construction? Our existing knowledge of history? The label? The catalogue?	Clothes? Architecture? Style? Our existing knowledge of history and painting? Where it is displayed? The label? The catalogue? What is happening? Some object in the picture? The artist?
Where was it made?	In this country? In a studio? In a workshop? In a town? In the country? In a house? In a factory? At home?	In this country? In another country? In a studio? In a workshop? Indoors? Outside? In a house? In the country?
How has it changed since it was first made?	Are there signs of damage? Is it worn? Has it been repaired?	Is it faded? Are there signs of damage? Has it been restored? Has it been cut?
What is unusual/unique about it?	The decoration? The stitching? The fact that it has survived? Information about the wearer?	The colour? The composition? The style? What people are doing? The scale? The medium?
What interests you about it?	The shape? The decoration? The size? The differences from shoes today? Something you recognise? Something unfamiliar? Something familiar? The colours?	The sense of movement? The people's expressions? What is happening? The colours? The style? The way it is hung? The medium?
How does it make you feel?	Interested? Curious? Excited? Happy? Sad? Positive? Negative? Angry? Indifferent? Disturbed?	Excited? Interested? Curious? Happy? Sad? Positive? Negative? Angry? Indifferent? Disturbed?
Why is it in a museum or gallery?	Because it is so rare? Because it is so typical? Because it is beautiful? Because it was given to the museum? Because it is so valuable?	Because it is so rare? Because it is so typical? Because it is beautiful? Because it was given the the museum? Because it is so valuable? Because it shows something important?
What other questions would you like to ask?	When was it worn? How long was it used for? What did it cost to make?	How was it reviewed? What is it worth now? What other information is known about it?
How would you go about finding out more?	In the archive? Using catalogues? In other museums? In reference books?	In the archives? In other galleries? In the the catalogue? In reference books?

129

Closed questions can also be used when looking at paintings. The following questions, which are taken from worksheets used in Swansea at War, are closed questions

What is the painting about?
What materials has the artist used?
Is the paint flat or textured?

Later, they move from closed ones to more speculative and open ended ones

Which part of the painting do you think the artist wants us to look at more carefully?
How do you think the artist achieved this?
What does this painting remind you of?
How could the painting be improved?
('Looking at Paintings', Worksheets 1 and 2, in *The Art in Wales Collection Education Pack,*
Site Education, Swansea, no date)

Open ended questions allow for more than one answer, encourage imaginative speculation, problem solving, prediction, judgement making and, frequently, a personal response. They encourage students to explore the object by using words like 'might' or 'think' or 'guess' which imply that it is okay to have a go at the question even though you don't 'know' the answer. These words can be used to make daunting closed questions like 'What is it made of?' into something that more students might be prepared to answer. 'What do you think it might be made of?' is a much less intimidating question.

Both closed and open ended questions were used in the children's leaflet *Beginners' Guide to Braque* that accompanied the exhibition, *Braque, the Late Works.*

The stove

Braque and his wife could only keep the kitchen and bathroom heated. This painting shows the stove that Braque had used to warm his studio (the room where he made his pictures).

Look at the coal bucket in front of the stove, which is empty because there is no coal. Imagine being a bird standing still and looking at the bucket from the floor ... now fly above it.

The education team at London's Royal Academy used Braque's painting of the stove in a corner of his studio in their booklet, *Beginners' Guide to Braque.* They designed questions that would help students to focus their looking and thinking.

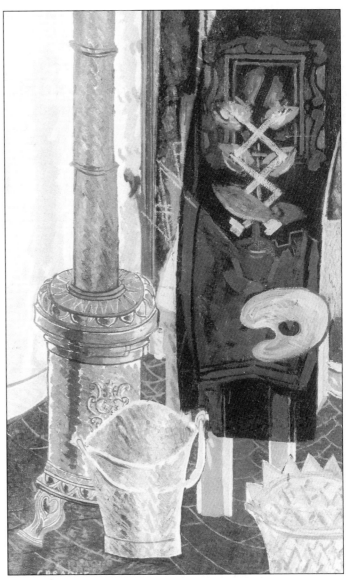

Yale University Art Gallery. Gift of Paul Rosenberg and Company in memory of Paul Rosenberg.

Why do you think Braque has painted both views at the same time?

How has he painted the table? Are you in front of it or looking down on it? Can you guess what the pale brown shape on the table might be?

Here relevant background information has been given to help students find answers or, in a sense, questions have been answered in the informative text. The written guide is designed to be interactive like a live guide or teacher and to encourage focused looking and thinking, keeping the student on the planned track.

The same technique can be used in discussion sessions

Elizabeth:	*It's yellow underneath but the actual colour is silver*
Teacher:	*What do you think the yellow material is?*
Jason:	*It's, it's ...*
David:	*Is it metal?*
Teacher:	*Well done. It is a metal called brass. Sometimes you see door handles and light switches made of brass.*
David:	*The thingy what you bang on our front door's made of that stuff*
Teacher:	*The door knocker. Yes mine is made of brass too. The telescope is made of brass and then it is covered with a thin layer of another metal. Can anyone think why?*
Elizabeth:	*To protect it. Does the silver wash off?*

(Sue Wilkinson and John Yoruth, 1996)

Students should be asked about the basis upon which they have answered questions and drawn their conclusions. Their answers should be frequently followed up by the additional question 'why...?' so that other members of the group can understand the reasoning or supposition behind an answer.

Much of the work that takes place in museums and galleries involves students answering questions. However, students should also be encouraged to ask their own questions of the objects and of each other. Objects are very good at stimulating questions. We found that our focus group participants continually asked each other questions and thought out loud

> *It's a banker's wife here in London – a socialite who has an artistic circle. The dress she is wearing is in the Museum of London. She didn't have very good taste, did she? It would be nice to get the dress alongside the painting. Does the painting do the dress justice? It would make her more real wouldn't it? The dress would be quite floppy really. You'd need the corset as well. I think it would expose the picture as being an artifice – a construct of the artist's imagination. It would really look so different on the body. Is it an honest portrayal? Are any portraits? Is it idealised? She's no great beauty is she? She looks like a good, solid bourgeois to me. I don't think he's made her look anything that she wasn't.* (Focus group, Leighton House)

Participants used what they already knew to pose questions to further their discussion. They responded to each other with answers, supposition or more questions.

Trying to find out how and why things worked, in this case a ratchet candle, also stimulated questions

133

> *The logic of how things worked was interesting. To lower it is tricky but to raise it you can do it with one hand. We were speculating about why you needed to be able to do this. Did you need to do it quickly to move it out of the way when friends arrived? Or was it about reading? It couldn't have been on the wall because it would have been too close. Did they have shades? No. With candles they would have to have metal and that would cut the light out. It would be hung on a ratchet. Didn't you pull it down to light it? Didn't they have the same mechanism for pots over the fire? You had snuffers to put the candles out. Why did they bother with this technology? Couldn't they have climbed on a chair to light it? You don't need the ratchet but somebody thought you did. So, is it one of those utterly useless inventions? But it is useful to be able to have the light low for somebody reading. Then if it was over a table you could raise it for the family meal. But why not just put the candle on a different shelf? Did you change the height as the candle burnt down? Especially if you were carrying it about so that your hand didn't get burnt.* (Focus group, Museum of London)

Photo © Tate, London 2000

134

Left: Millais' portrait of Mrs. Bishoffsheim provoked many questions about 'reality' and the portrait painter's role during the brainstorming session at Leighton House.

Opposite: By contrast (with the portrait of Mrs. Bishoffsheim) this ratchet candle is an everyday utilarian object. However, because we all live with electric light, the focus group asked themselves simple, basic questions about its form and function.

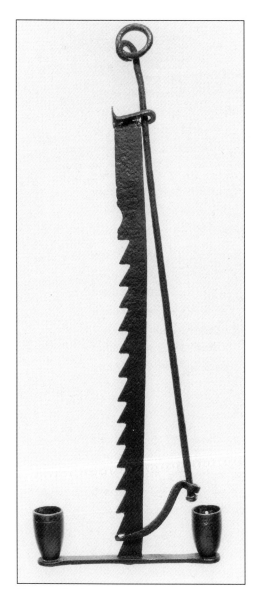

Museum of London

Finding the answers

Planning a museum or gallery visit should therefore include devising appropriate questions, some simple, some challenging, which will stimulate discussion and enable students to respond and find out for themselves.

However, teachers also need to provide themselves with some answers and relevant background information that will help them guide the session and keep to their chosen topic or theme. Knowing the answers makes for security in what might be an unfamiliar, public teaching situation. Teachers and educators should not be afraid of saying, in the spirit of the museum visit, 'I don't know but I can find out. How do you think I might do that?'

When open ended questions are planned, it is wise to be prepared for a range of answers and divergent thinking. Unexpected answers might be valuable and illuminating, adding to the excitement of the day and teachers should be open to some changes in direction. However, it is their task to keep answers securely embedded in their chosen topic or theme and, most importantly, to ensure they are related to the object which is the focus for the discussion in hand. Students should be asked to justify their answers.

Practical Work

Practical work might simply take the form of exploring and recording an image or object by drawing or writing. The experience of looking, discovery and discussion might well be cemented in the mind by this, but there are also other means such as drama, dance, photography or making things

135

which can also serve as ways of recording the experience of the visit and taking the project forward in some way.

During *Greek Vase*, students made drawings of 18th century Wedgwood pots inspired by classical Greece, as well as of the ancient Greek vase itself which was the focus of the story that they developed and wrote up later. In the museum, as an additional, more important, aide memoir and record, the education officer gave them flash card vocabularies of European place names, modes of transport and places where travellers might stay

> *Of course, these could be extended, but the idea was that the children would work in groups and cut off the cards to match the story they wished to write. They would write about their quest for the pot from the standpoint of the character they had been given at the museum – servant, aristocrat, ship keeper, innkeeper or archaeologist (Greek Vase)*

For *The Egyptians*, which linked art, technology, PSE, RE and English, the art education officer gave a short talk about ancient Egyptian attitudes to death, memorials and the spirit world, and linked these to the work of a contemporary artist. Year 10 students then drew Egyptian objects. They were asked to capture their flavour through greatly enlarging small objects in their charcoal or pastel drawings and to write down a list of words about those they had chosen. All this was used later as the basis for discussion. Their words were put together on a flip chart '*so that they had a word picture of the group's experience in the Egyptian gallery*'

The art education officer also

> *returned to the notion of objects having a spiritual value for the living and the dead and suggested ways of taking this forward into their own work. She asked them about objects in their possession such as lucky charms or iconic images that had special meaning and resonance for them – a preciousness that did not relate to monetary value...She ended with the idea that they should make something about themselves and of value to themselves that they would like to take with them into the next world.*

The whole experience was further cemented in school by the task of making reference sheets of design ideas using visual reminders from the museum's packs, postcards and posters,

136

before embarking on Art and Design work using a range of two and three dimensional materials.

During their visit to the exhibition *Braque, the Late Works* students did no practical work at all, this being reserved for class work. On the other hand, in *Art and Dance*, practical dance activity on site was used both as exploration and as the final product of the day's work. For the under fives who worked on *Splash!* the process of making the exhibition and its interpretation for other visitors provided both practical work and a record of their experience.

Ending the session

At the end of discussion or at the end of the practical component of the session, if one is planned, time should be allowed for a review of what has been seen, discovered and learnt. Summing up should relate to previous class work, experience and knowledge as well as the students' recent experience in the gallery. Although it should be a unique experience, the museum or gallery visit should not be isolated from the school curriculum.

And now they can visit the shop.

137

Abbreviations and Acronyms

ACE	Arts Council of England
ACGB	Arts Council of Great Britain
CC	Crafts Council
DCMS	Department for Culture, Media and Sport
DES	Department for Education and Science
DfEE	Department for Education and Employment
DNH	Department of National Heritage
DT	Design and Technology
EMU	Education for Mutual Understanding (Northern Ireland)
engage	National Association for Gallery Education
GEM	Group for Education in Museums
INSET	In-Service Training
JADE	Journal of Art and Design Education
KS	Key Stage
LEA	Local Education Authority
MGC	Museums and Galleries Commission
NACCCE	National Advisory Committee on Creativity and Cultural Education
NPG	National Portrait Gallery
NSEAD	National Society for Education in Art and Design
OFSTED	Office for Standards in Education
PSE	Personal and Social Education
QCA	Qualifications and Curriculum Authority
RE	Religious Education
Resource	Resource: The Council for Museums, Archives and Libraries
SEARCH	The Search Centre, 50 Clarence Road, Gosport PO12 1BU. Run by Hampshire County Council's Museums Service
SELB	Southern Education and Library Board (Northern Ireland)
SEMEU	South East Museums Education Unit

Bibliography

Listed alphabetically by the surname of the first author. Government reports, which have no designated author, are listed in title order]

Alive with Learning – Study support in museums and galleries, Education Extra, 1999

All our Futures: Creativity, culture and education, National Advisory Committee on Creativity and Cultural Education and Department for Education and Employment, 2000

David Anderson, *A Common Wealth: Museums and learning in the United Kingdom*, Department for National Heritage, 1997. 2nd edition 1999. Available from The Stationery Office

Rob Barnes, 'Getting the Act Together: it may be Cross-curricular, but is it Really Art?', *Journal of Art and Design Education*, Vol 12, No1, 1993

Ray Batchelor 'Not looking at Kettles' (in Susan M Pearce, ed., *Interpreting Objects and Collections*, Routledge, 1994)

The Benefits of Study Support, A review of opinion and research, Department for Education and Employment, 1999. Available from DfEE

Norman Birch and Sue Clive, *Close collaborations: art in schools and the wider environment*, Arts Council of England/Trentham Books, 1994

Norman Birch and Liz Roberson, *Resourcing and Assessing Art, Craft and Design*, Arts Council of Great Britain, the Crafts Council and NSEAD, 1994

Children as an Audience for Museums and Galleries, Arts Council of England and Museums and Galleries Commission, 1997

Sue Clive and Petra Geggie, *Unpacking Teachers' Packs*, **engage**, London, 1998

Dingy Places and Different Kinds of Bits, London Museums Service, 1991

Gail Durbin, Susan Morris and Sue Wilkinson, *A Teachers' Guide to Learning from Objects*, English Heritage, 1990. Available from English Heritage

Extending Opportunities: A national framework for study support, Department for Education and Employment, 1998. Available from DfEE

R Fransecky and J Debbs, *Visual Literacy: A way to learn, a way to read,* US Association for Education, Communication and Technology, 1972

Paulo Friere and Donald Macedo, *Reading the Word and the World*, Massachusetts, (Bergin and Garvey Inc), 1987

Group of Large Local Authority Museums, (London), 2000

John Harland and Kay Kinder, eds., *Crossing the Line: Extending young people's access to cultural venues*, Calouste Gulbenkian Foundation, (London) 1999

The Learning Power of Museums; A vision for museum education, 2000. Department for Culture Media and Sport and Department for Education and Employment Available from DCMS

A National Strategy for Neighbourhood Renewal, The Social Exclusion Unit, 2000

Karen Raney, *Visual Literacy: Issues and debates*, Middlesex University and Arts Council of Great Britain, 1997. Her quote is from the book by Fransecky and Debbs listed above.

A Survey of Schools' use of Resources, Department for Education and Science, 1992

Sue Wilkinson and John Yorath, *Going Interactive*, SEARCH, 1996

Visitors to Museums and Galleries in the United Kingdom, Museums and Galleries Commission, 2000

142